TAILS

FROM THE

BOOTH

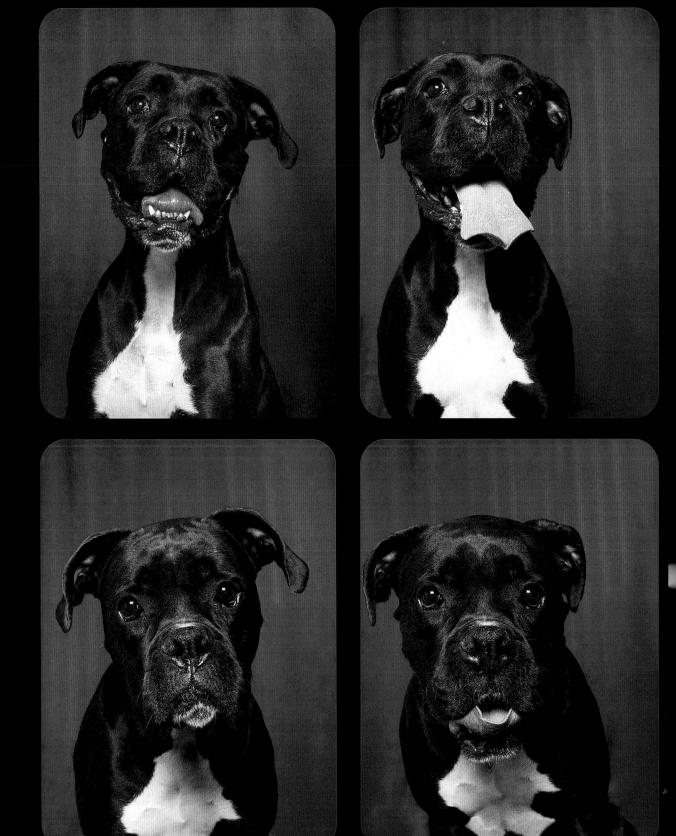

TAILS

FROM THE

BOOTH

LYNN TERRY

GALLERY BOOKS

NEW YORK   LONDON   TORONTO   SYDNEY   NEW DELHI

G

Gallery Books
An Imprint of Simon & Schuster, Inc.
1230 Avenue of the Americas
New York, NY 10020

First Gallery Books hardcover edition October 2015

GALLERY BOOKS and colophon are registered trademarks of Simon & Schuster, Inc.

For information about special discounts for bulk purchases, please contact Simon &
Schuster Special Sales at 1-866-506-1949 or business@simonandschuster.com.

The Simon & Schuster Speakers Bureau can bring authors to your live event. For
more information or to book an event, contact the Simon & Schuster Speakers
Bureau at 1-866-248-3049 or visit our website at www.simonspeakers.com.

Interior design by Jill Putorti

Manufactured in the United States of America

10 9 8 7 6 5 4 3 2

Library of Congress Cataloging-in-Publication Data

Terry, Lynn.
  Tails from the booth / Lynn Terry.
    pages cm
   ISBN 978-1-5011-0069-7 (hardback)—ISBN 978-1-5011-0070-3 (ebook)
1. Dogs—Pictorial works. I. Title.
  SF430.T48 2015
  636.70022'2—dc23
                            2015011235

ISBN 978-1-5011-0069-7
ISBN 978-1-5011-0070-3 (ebook)

This book is dedicated,
in gratitude and affection,
to the memory of my dog DeeDee.
It is because of you, sweet girl,
that I fell in love with dog-kind and
so began the true path to my career.

And to my dear husband and best friend, Luke,
and our cute pup of a daughter, Adelaide,
without whom this book would have been
completed so very much sooner.

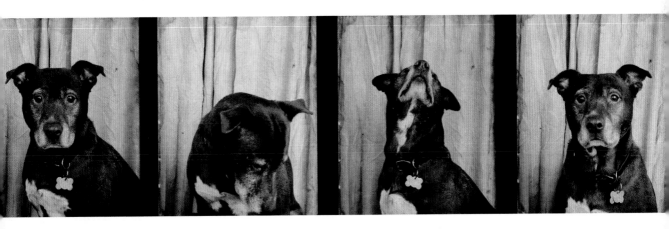

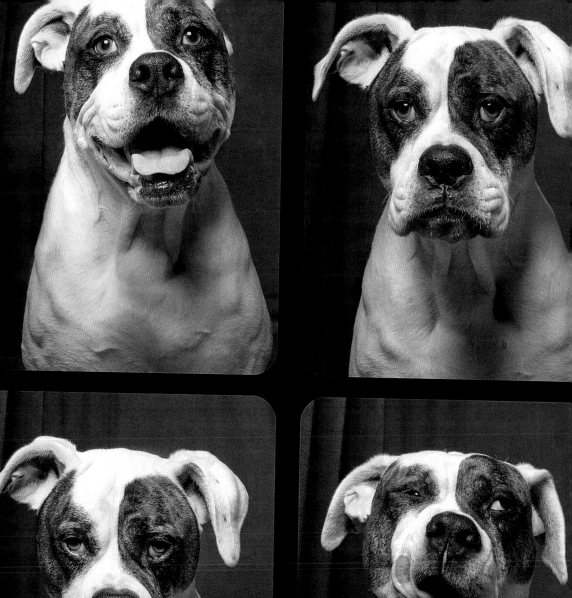

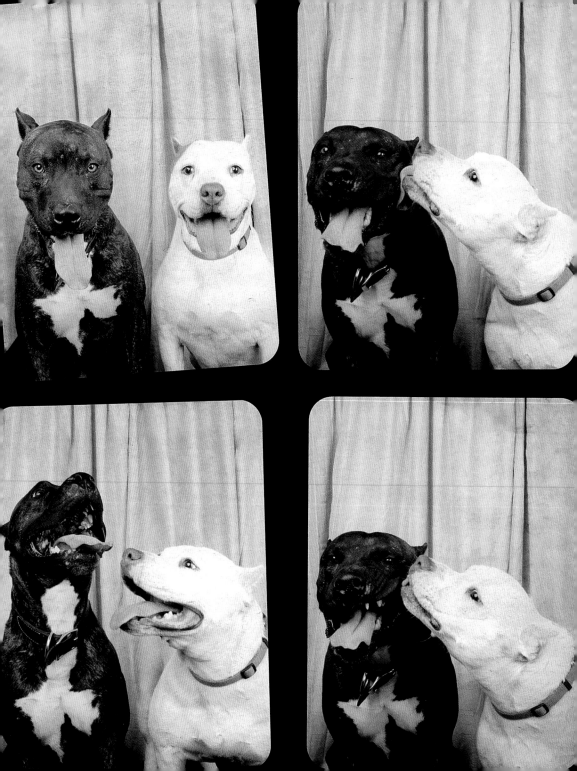

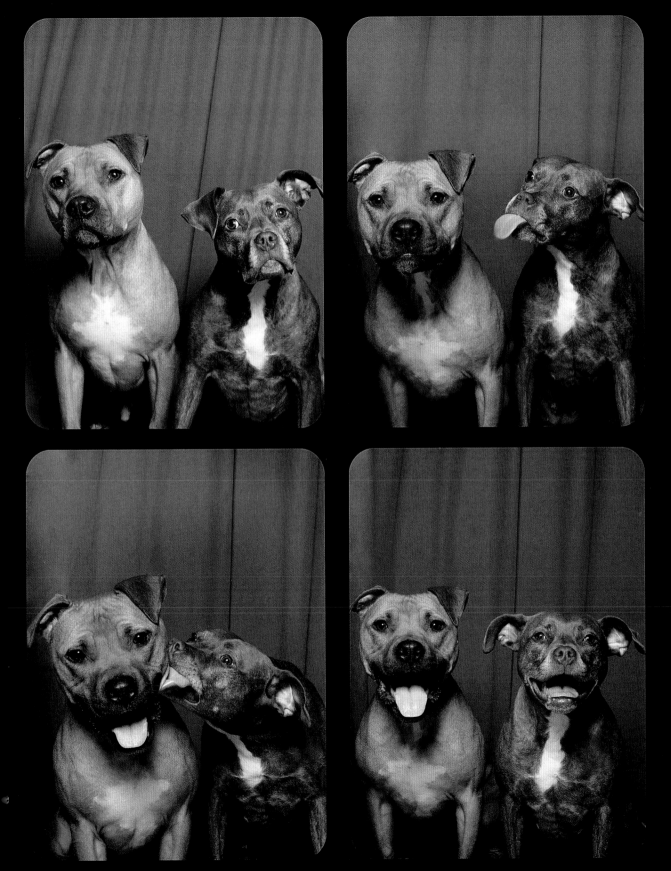

MY TALE OF THE BOOTH

One would surmise, by viewing my other photography or visiting my home, that I have an interest in history and pretty much anything dating from before 1950: I live in a 104-year-old home, I collect antiques, I enjoy shooting pinup-style photography and have an entire wardrobe and props from that era. Old photographs of all my earliest ancestors are framed on my walls, among a collection of antique photos of dogs and humans together, peppered with a collection of anthropomorphic animal art.

In 2006, inspired by my obsession with vintage photos, I began a photo booth series of dogs for a local pit bull rescue group. I sat two dogs in front of some old curtains I had that reminded me of old photo booth drapes. The results were so much better than I expected! These two dogs were such great friends that I didn't need to use any of the tricks I'd learned over years of pet photography. The dogs automatically started licking each other, and upon editing, I realized how much they looked like young lovers sneaking in a little make out session behind the auditorium.

Everyone I shared it with loved this shot, so, flattered by all the interest people had expressed, I began experimenting with different backdrops and different dogs. I first built something out of PVC so that I could adjust the height based on the size of the dogs as well as transport it easily. I played around with this for a few years and then put the project aside. But in November of 2013, my beloved dog, DeeDee, passed away at age fifteen. I never took pictures of myself with her. I've since regretted it, so the following February, I organized an event to photograph people with their four-legged loves in the booth for Valentine's Day. Knowing how receptive people were to the original photo booth shots, I figured this would be a fun campaign.

Sure enough, these shots were a huge success too, and so began the process for the book.

My husband custom-built a more suitable photo booth for the dogs, with the same dimensions as a real booth. We surrounded it in curtains so that we had access to it from all sides but, if the well-behaved-dog gods saw fit, we could immerse them completely in a 100 percent genuine photo booth experience and seclude them. Using the real dimensions created the authentic look of a photo booth. The camera angle was always the same and the seating area was always consistent, so if they moved toward the lens or to the left or right, they were outside of the frame or out of focus, just like the real deal.

Each successive shoot kept producing amazing images. The more I did it the more amazed I became at the wonderful ways the dogs expressed themselves behind the curtain. They not only waited patiently for the camera once the curtains were drawn, they began interacting with each other in the same spontaneous way longtime friends do once the money is inserted and the countdown starts. Sure, the dogs didn't know they were being photographed, but it didn't matter. They were unable to resist socializing with one another and expressing their affection or curiosity.

The photos began capturing the personalities of the different breeds, the humor they shared in the photo booth, the friendship they projected and desired, their willingness to adapt and improvise, their innate sense of concern and wonder and love, and above all, their flawless parody of the human condition with all its warts and freckles. The dogs began sticking their tongues out at each other, laughing, yawning, howling, sneezing, frowning, making awkward facial expressions, walking out of the frame, etc. In a nutshell, they nailed it!

I was thrilled with the results from these shoots, but I couldn't have imagined what was going to happen next . . .

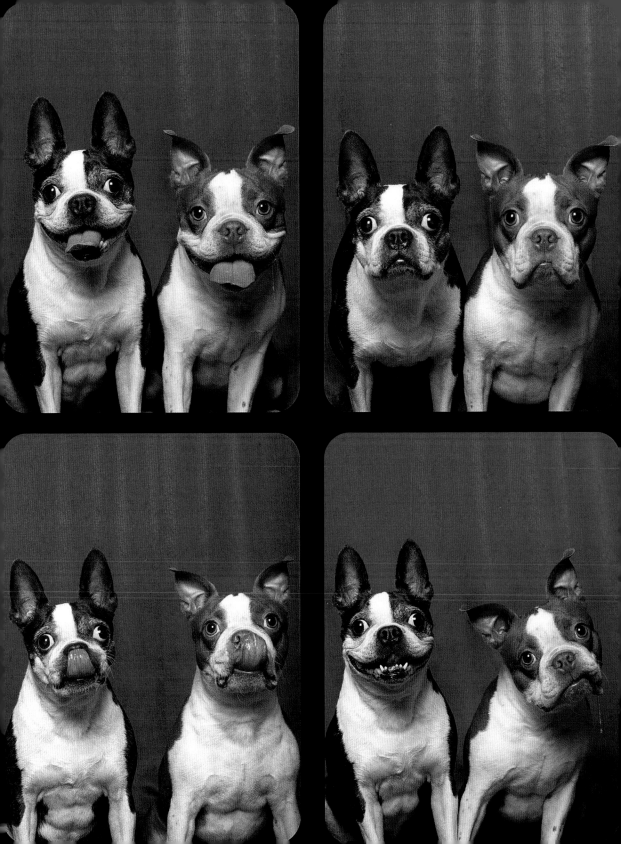

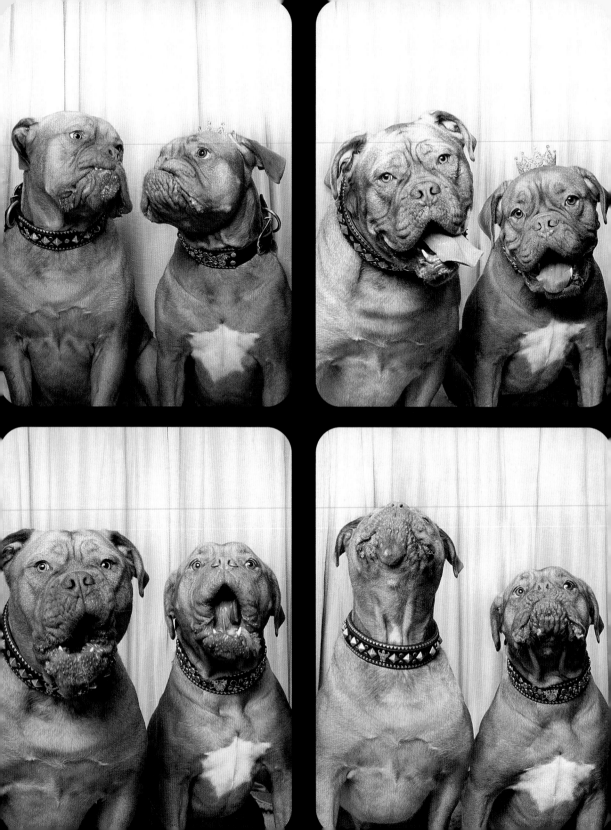

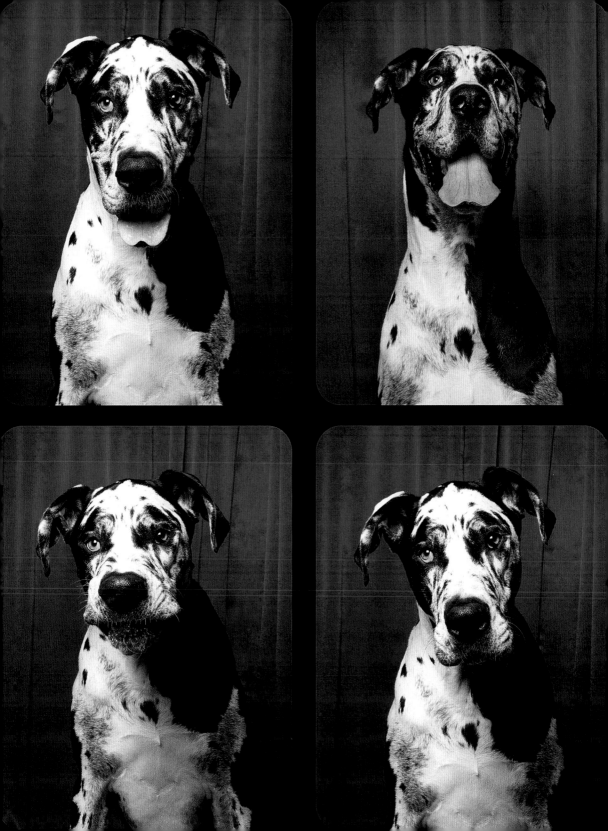

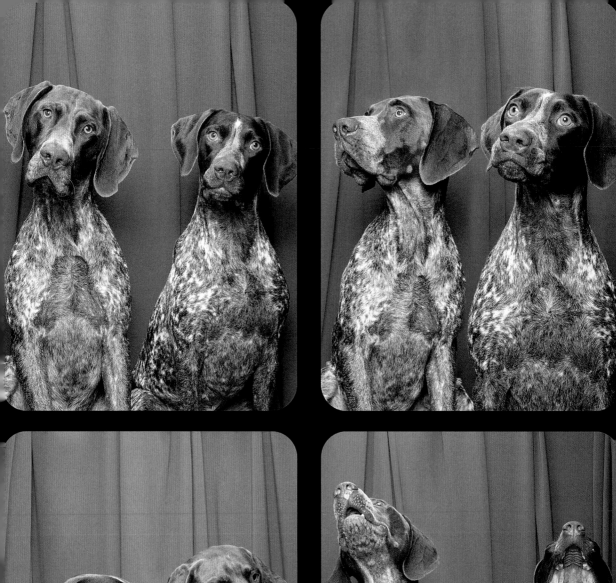
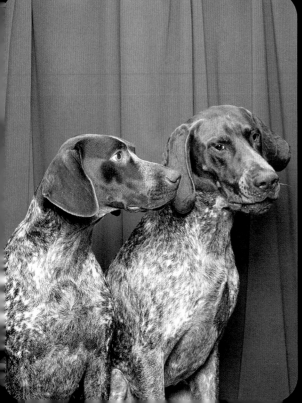
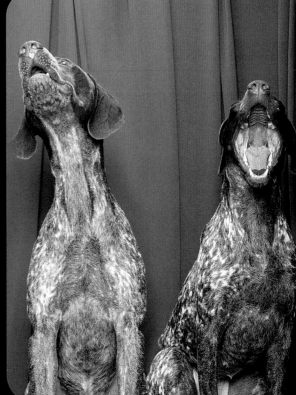

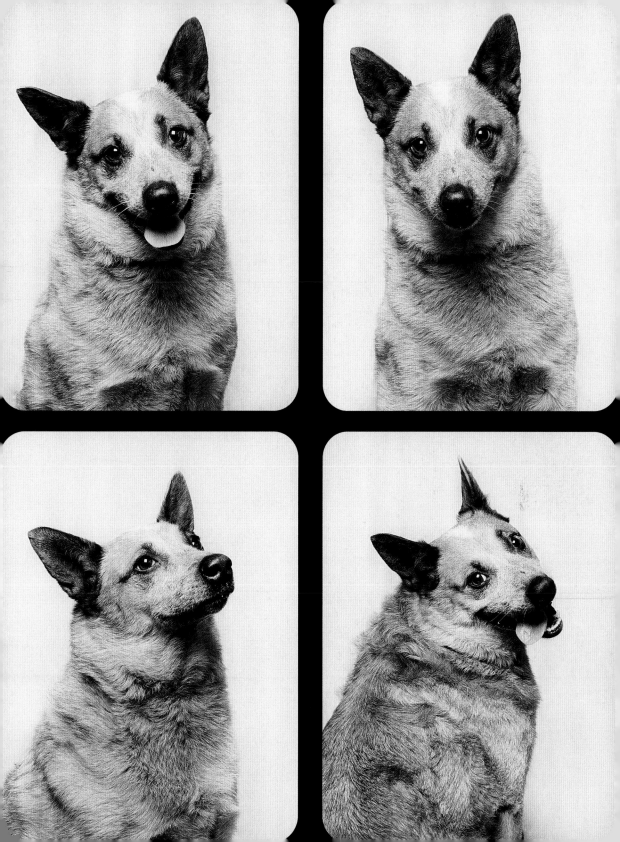

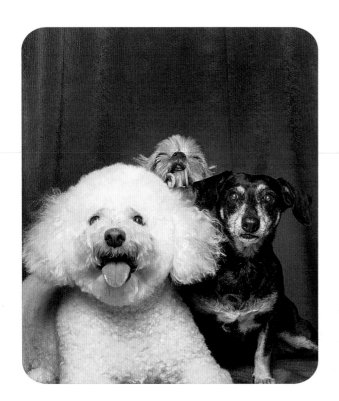 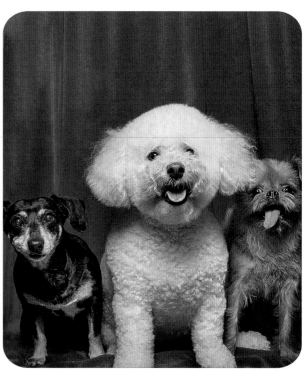

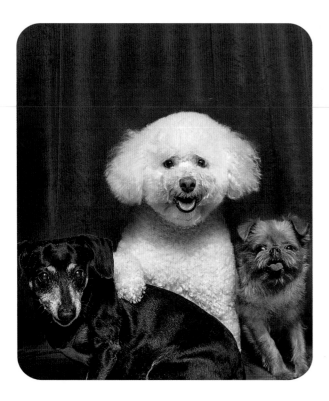 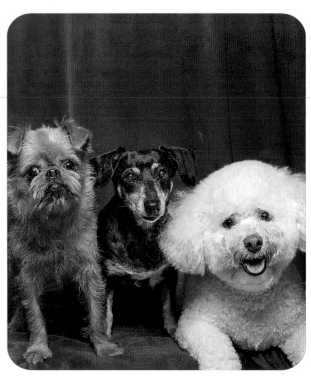

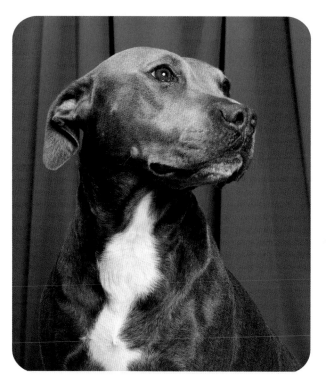
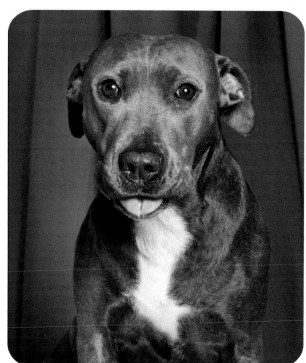
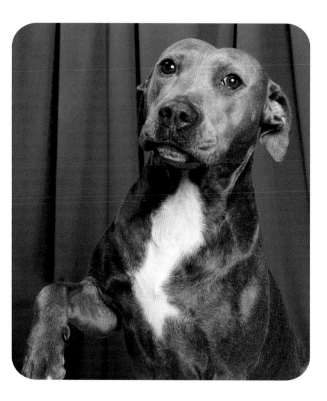
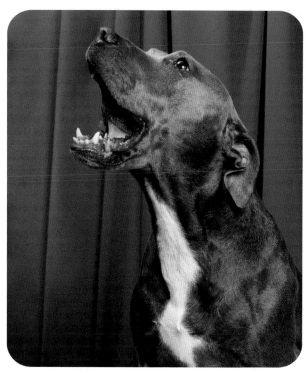

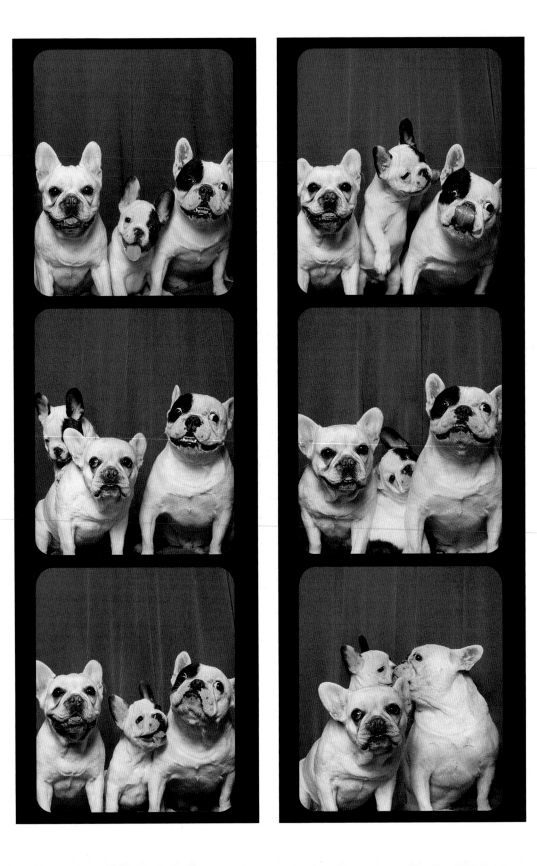

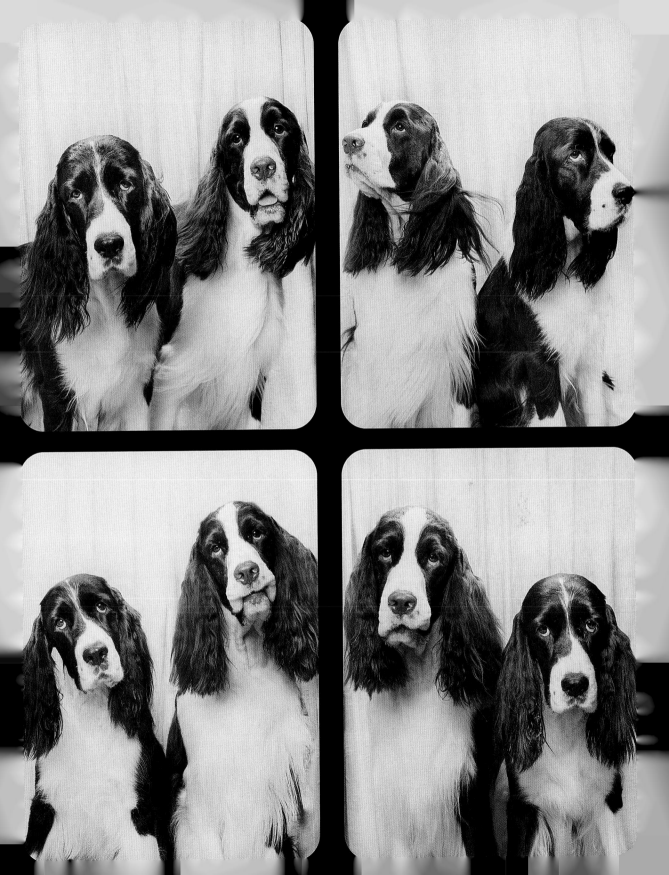

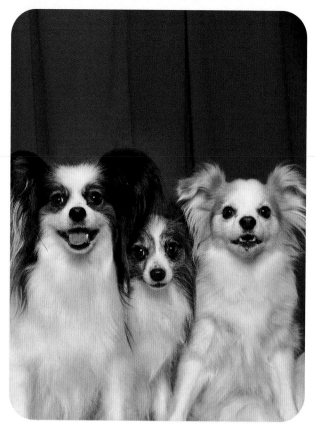
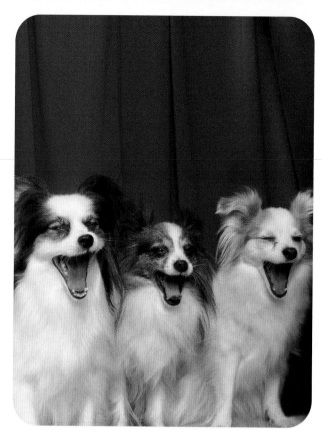
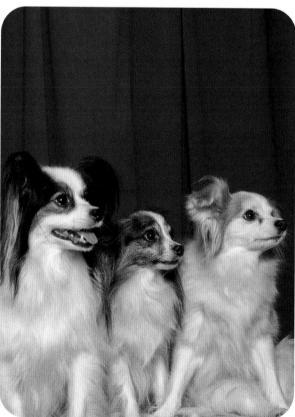
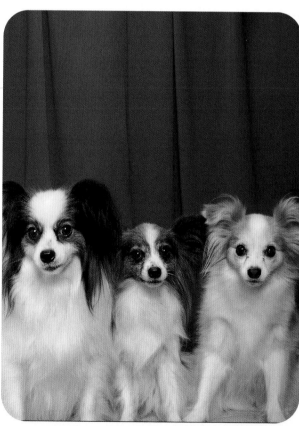

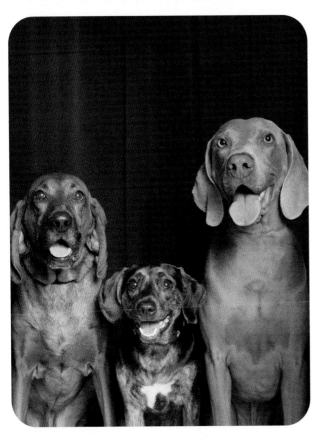
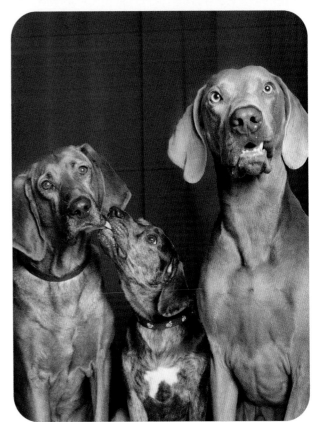
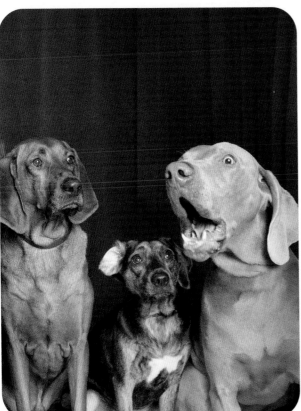
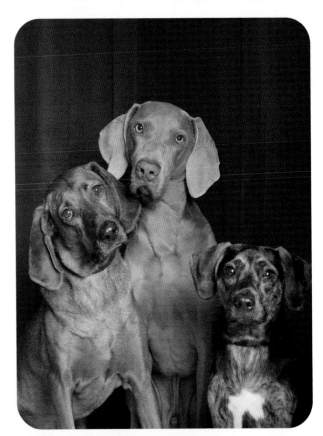

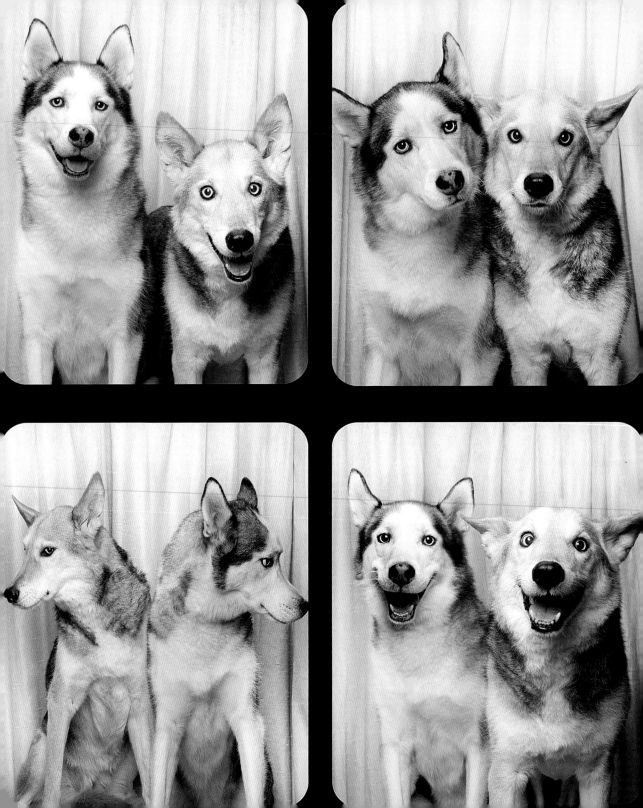

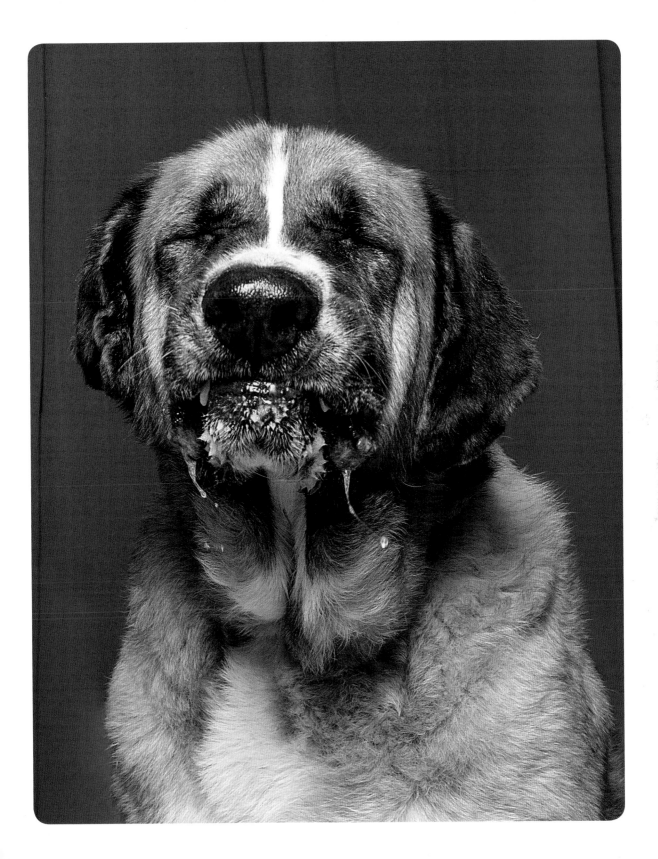

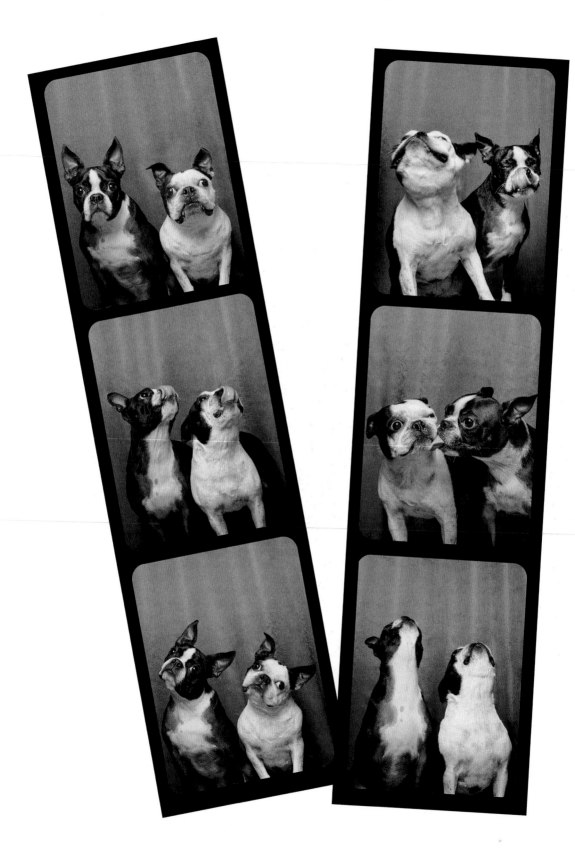

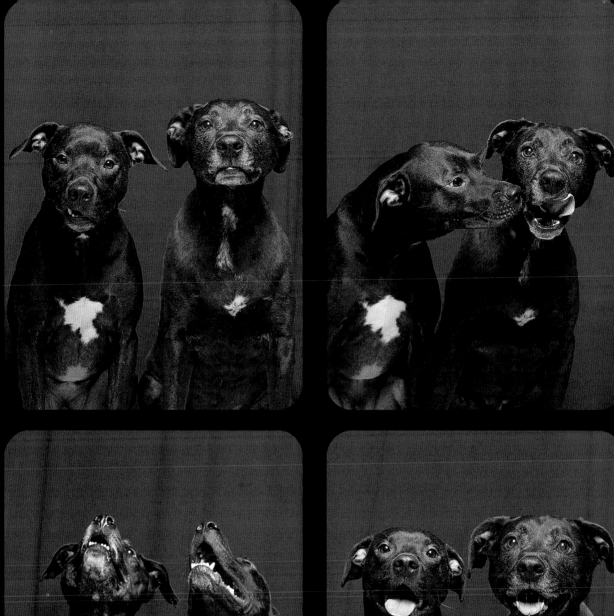
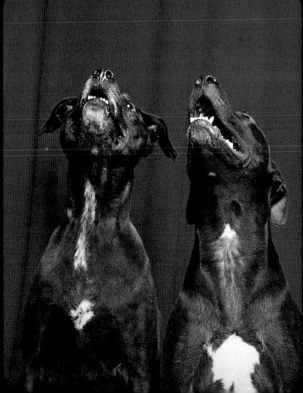
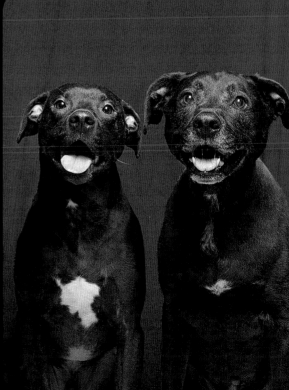

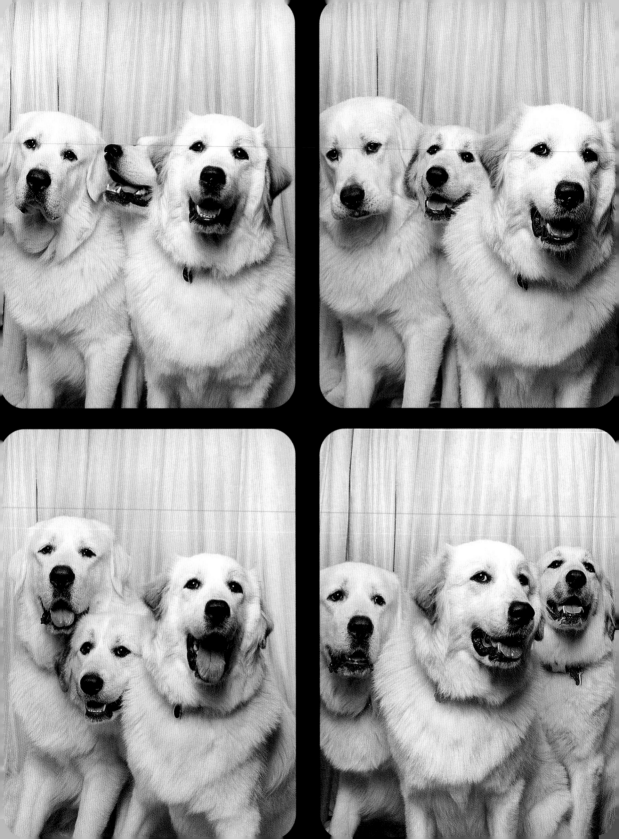

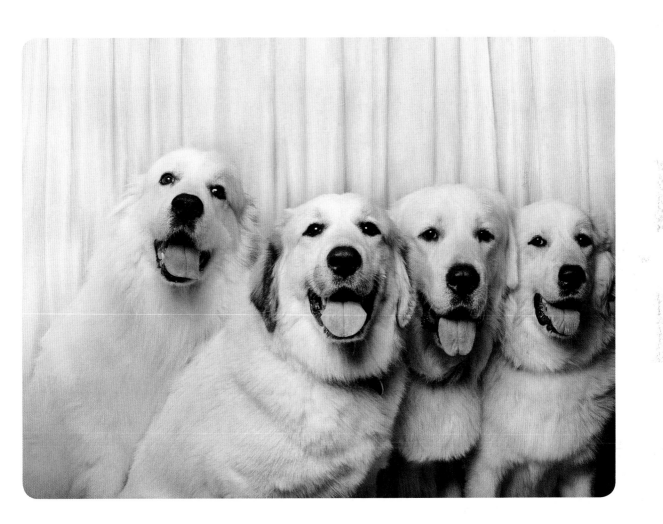

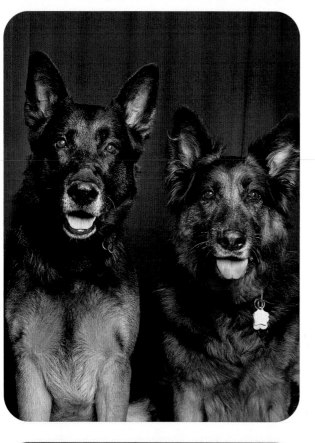
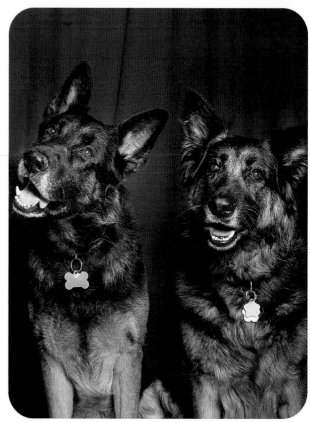
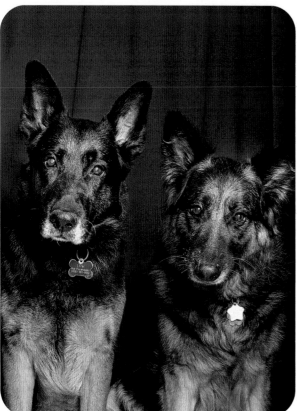
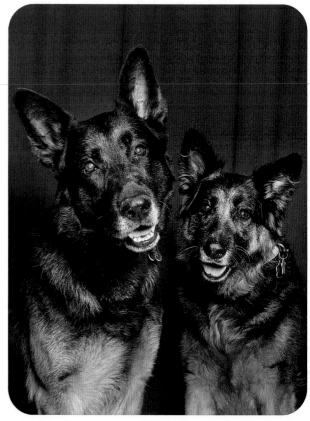

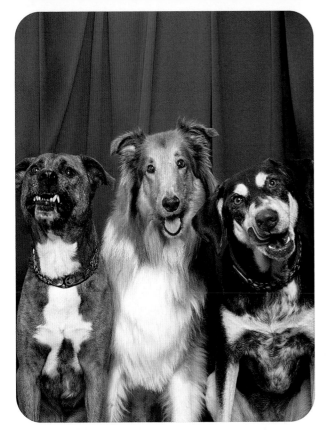

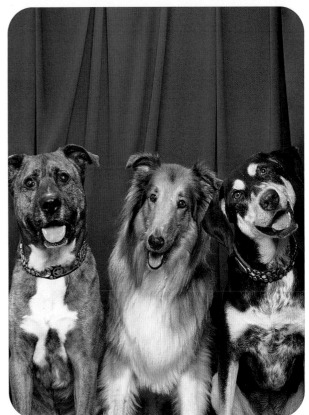

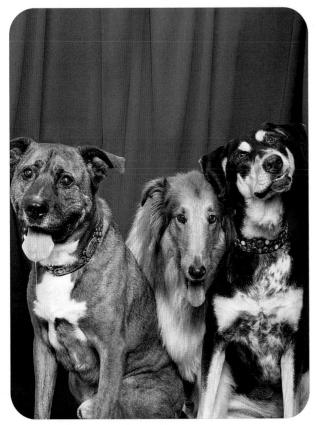

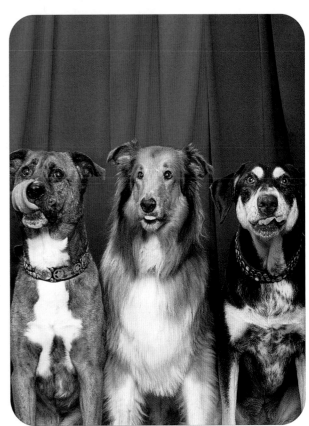

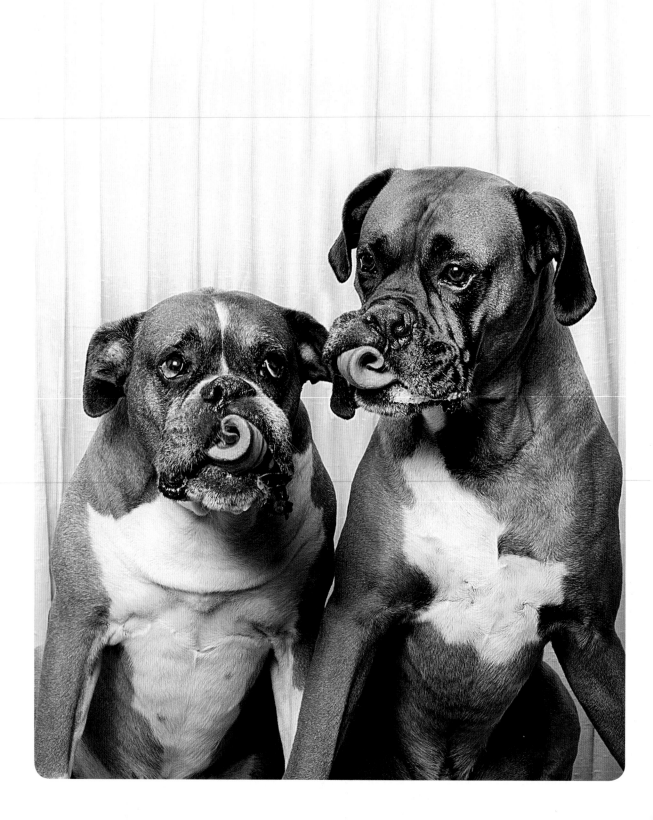

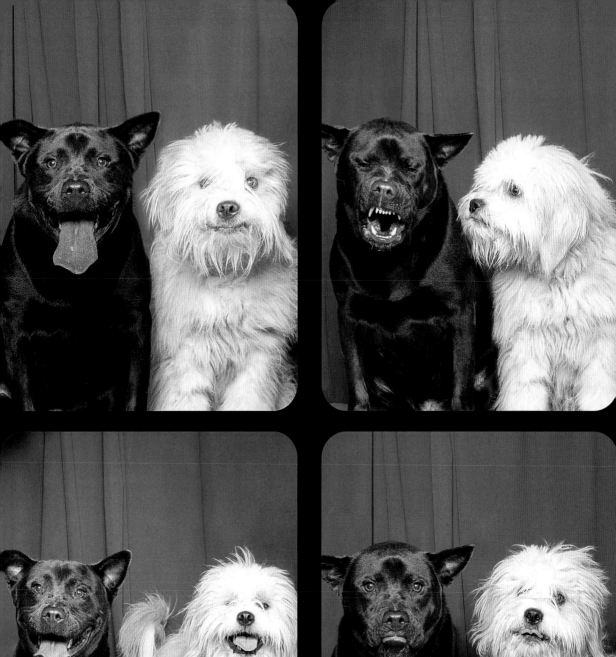

GOING VIRAL

The story goes like this. I arranged shots of two dogs licking and laughing with each other into a panel of four images and added borders and sepia tone for that "vintage" photo booth look. The set of photos just made me laugh, and I put it online, thinking that some of my clients might see it and enjoy it as well. To my surprise, it was an instant hit and began flying around the web—with no watermark. Periodically I would get e-mails telling me it was spotted on some website somewhere. Most of the time it was being used as a banner for a rescue group. I figured if it was helping a few dogs get adopted, then so be it, even though it was bittersweet to have created such a well-received image without anyone knowing it was mine.

As the original shot continued to grow in popularity, I decided to work on a new series. I jokingly advertised the project: "Create your own version of this iconic image with the anonymous original artist." I photographed a second series with two pit bulls and the moment I edited the photos together, I knew in my gut I had created an even more magical photo series than the original image that went viral. I sent the picture to the dogs' owner, and sure enough, within twenty-four hours my e-mail was blowing up.

I am not sure exactly how it got so big so fast, but I know that *Huffington Post* was the first to catch wind of the project, writing an article that received over 215,000 likes and was shared over 40,000 times within twenty-four hours. The series started appearing on some of the world's largest news sites, such as *ABC News, Today, People,* and *Good Morning America.* It was also re-blogged through influential culture websites such as Tumblr, Bored Panda, Pinterest, and Facebook. I received an outpouring of kind e-mails from people telling me how wonderful the photos were and how much they made their day. I read e-mail after e-mail from people sharing their own dog stories. Something about the intimacy of these images just encouraged people to reach out and tell me, a total stranger, about the dogs they loved like family. I had no idea how much one image could touch so many lives. I was completely humbled and honored.

Among the e-mails were messages from a few agents and publishers asking if I had ever considered writing a book. I was floored. People loved these images so much that they wanted a whole book? It was all becoming such a dream come true. Naturally, my answer to those agents and publishers was, of course!

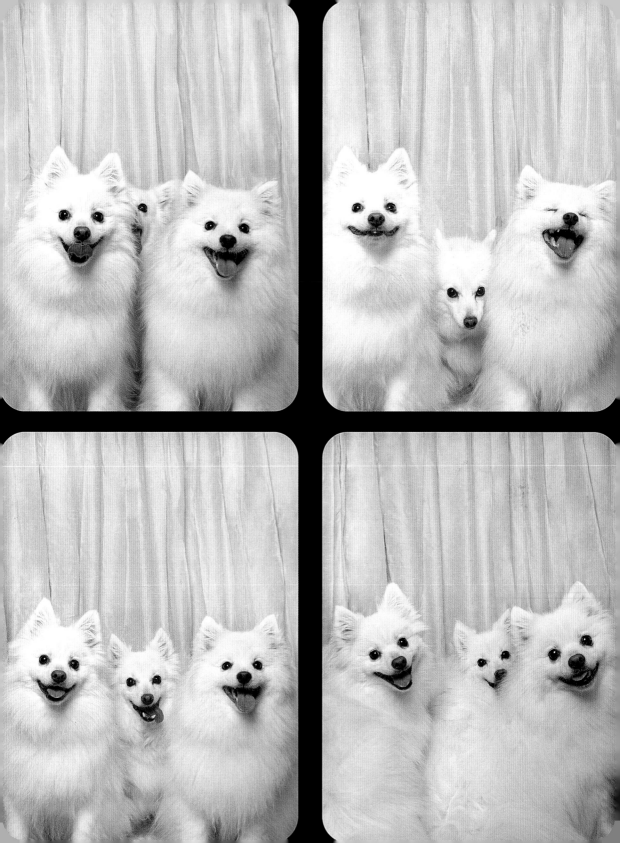

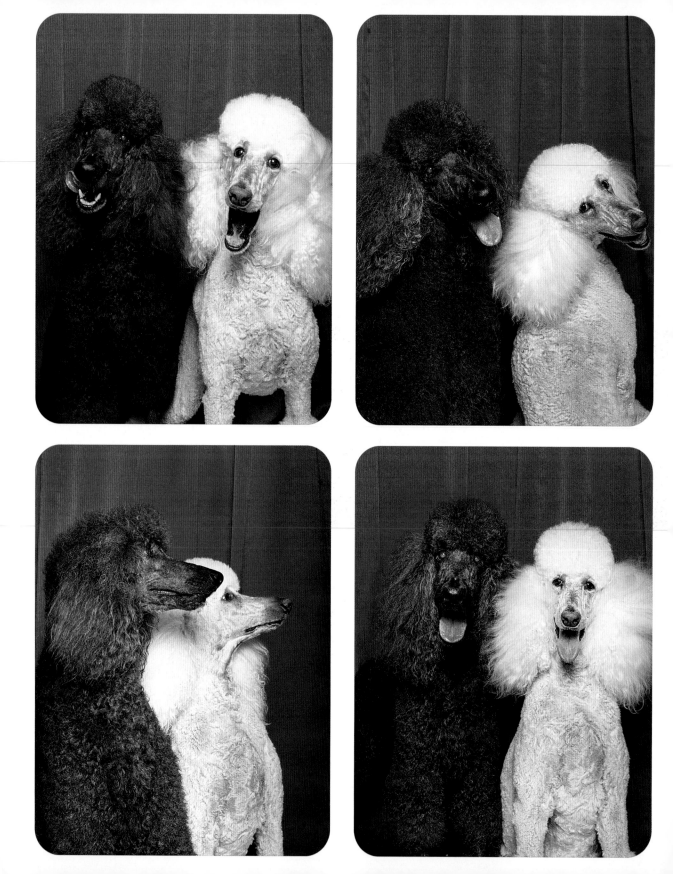

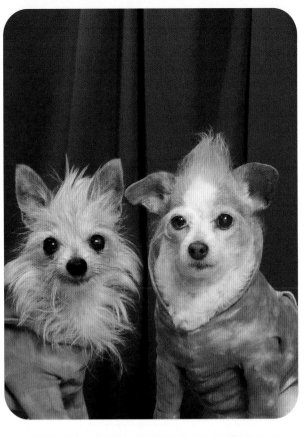
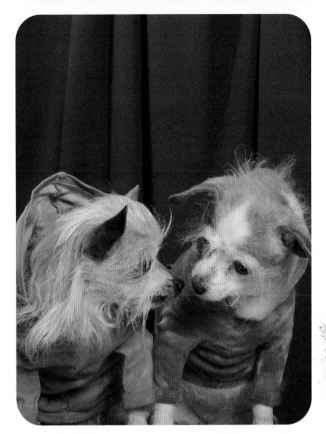
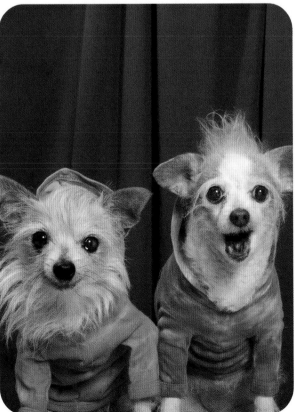
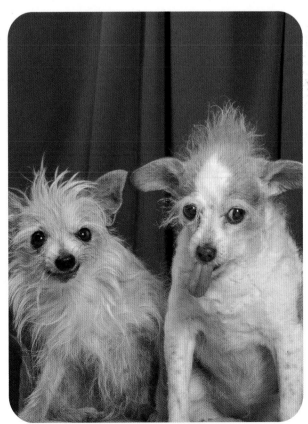

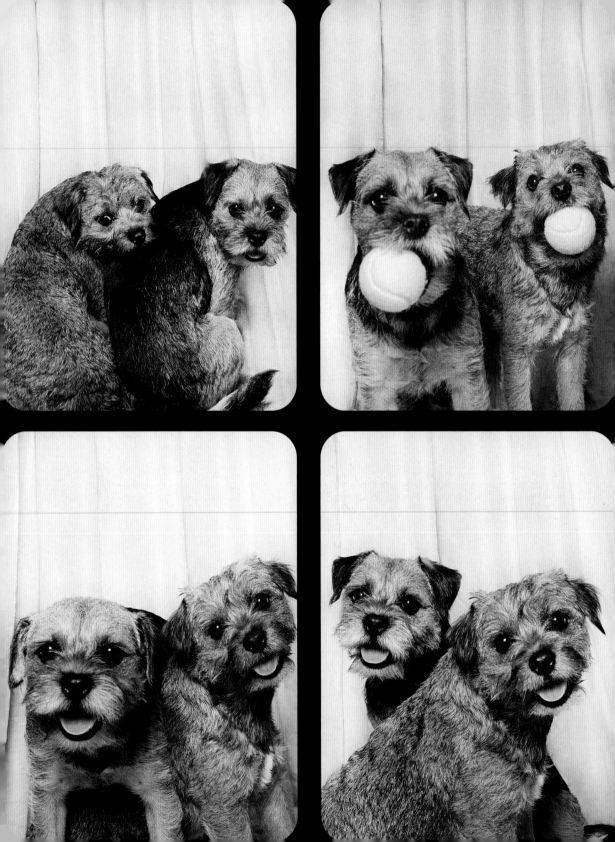

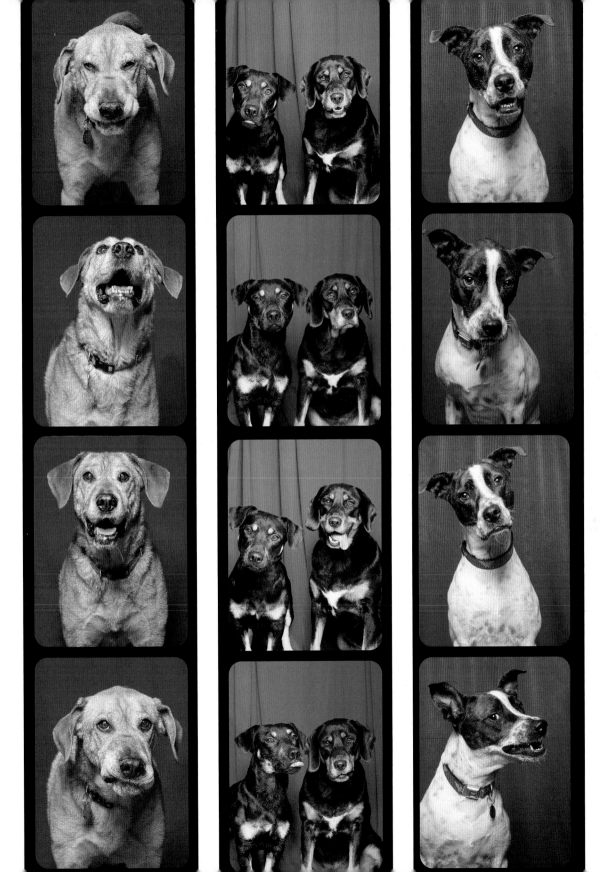

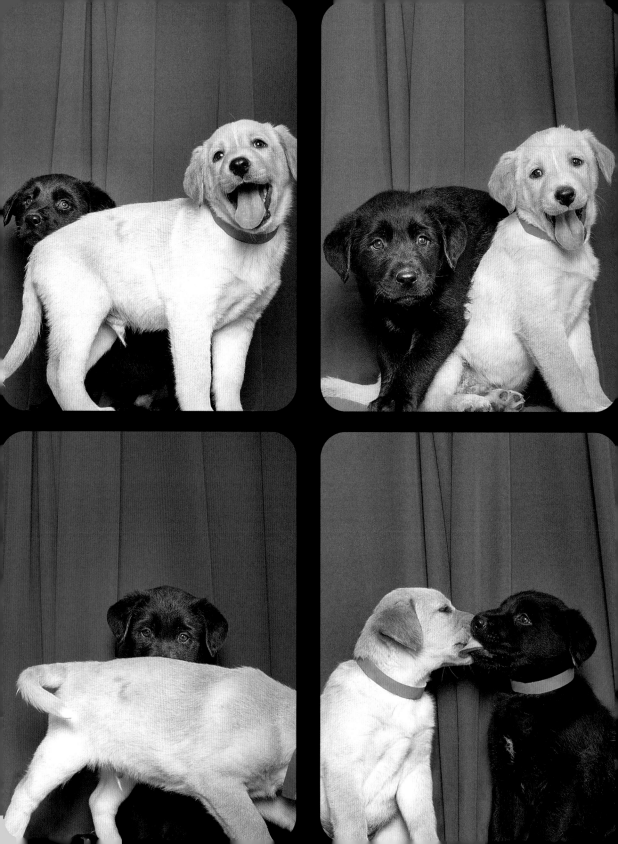

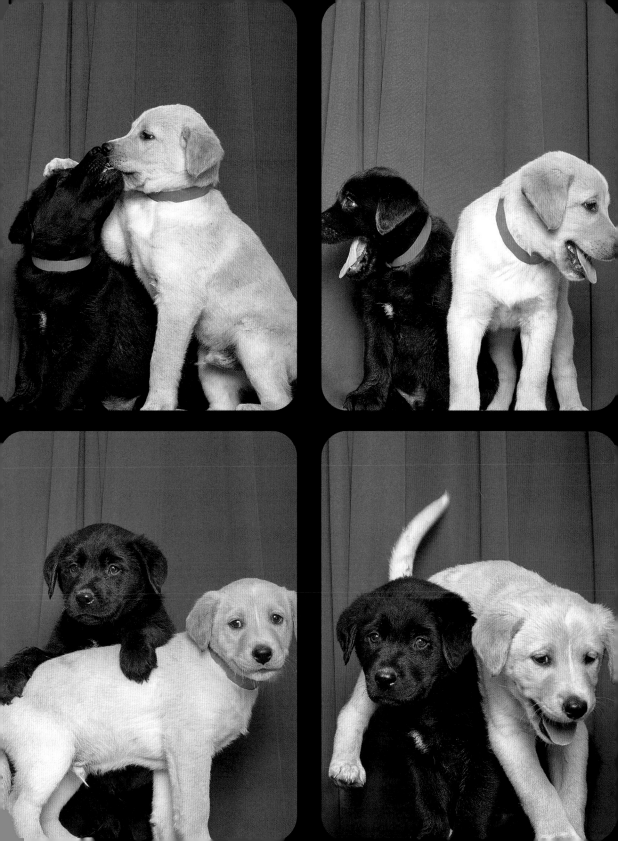

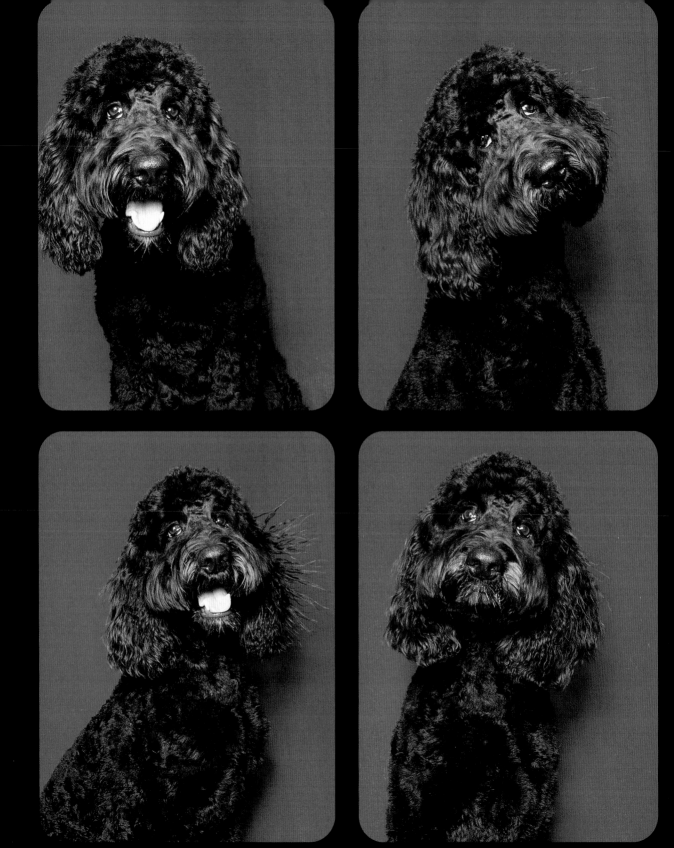

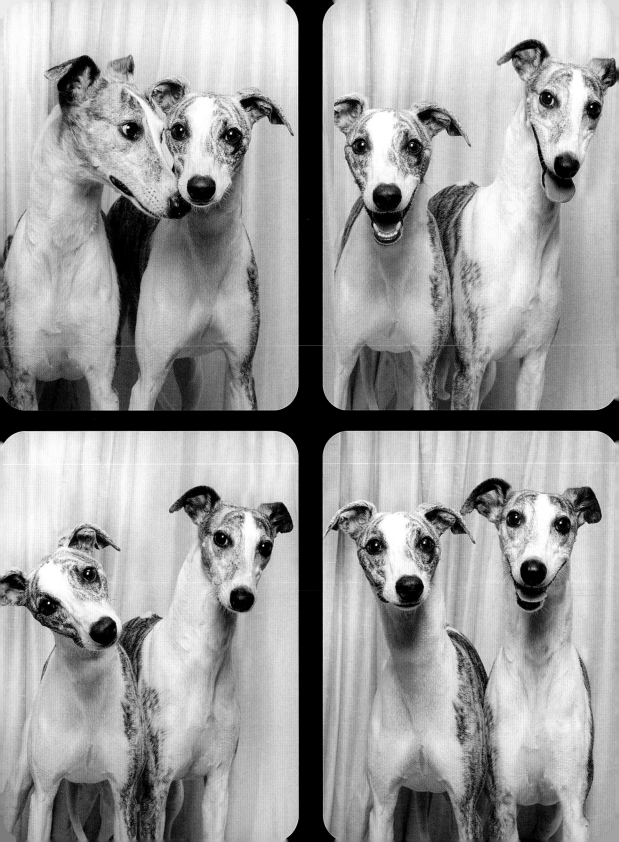

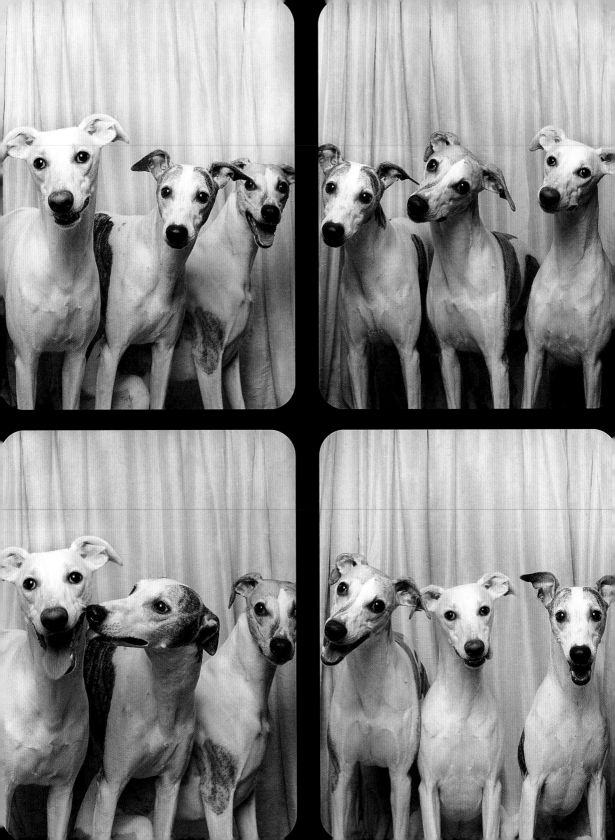

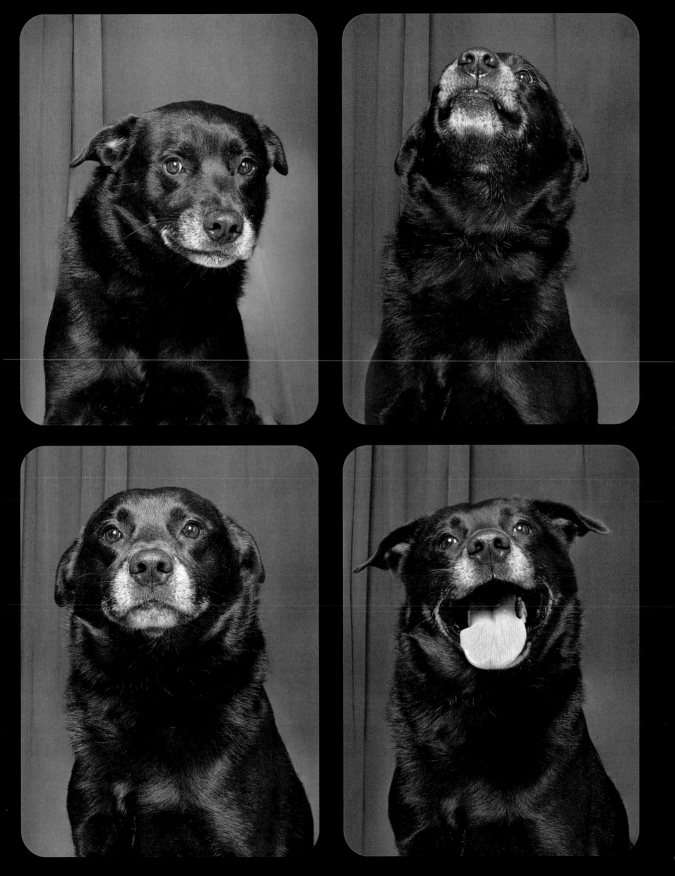

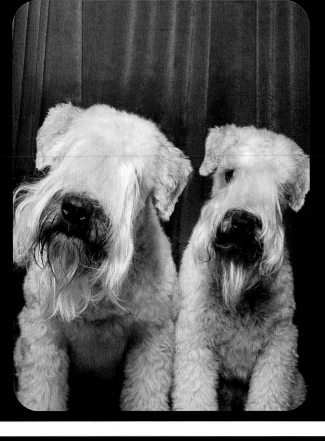
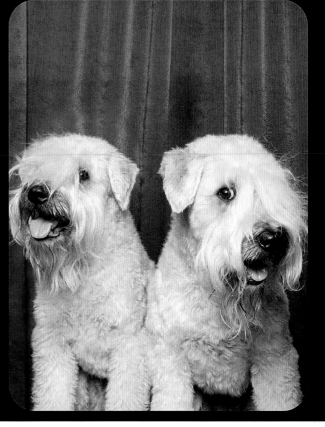
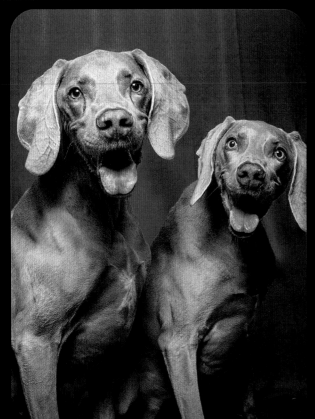
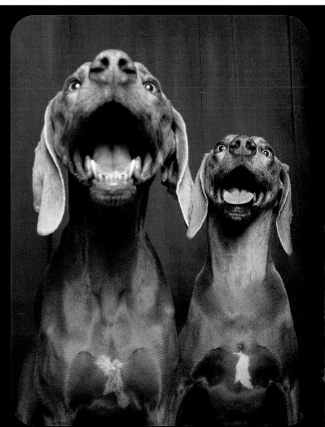

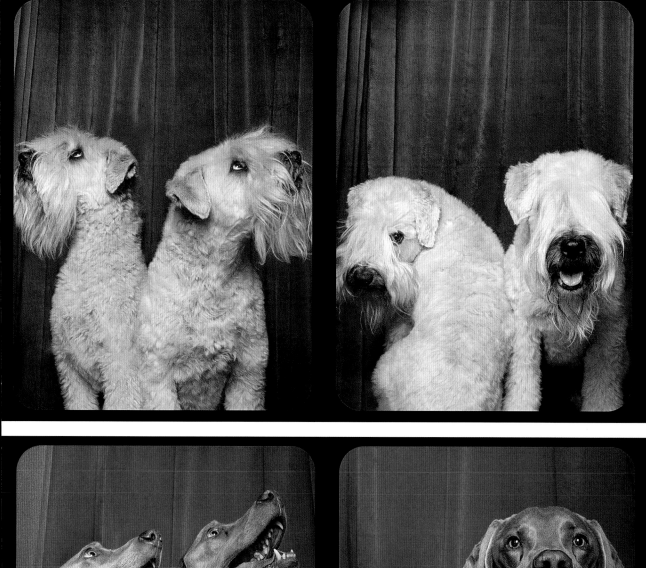

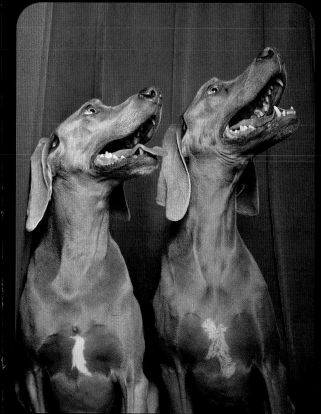

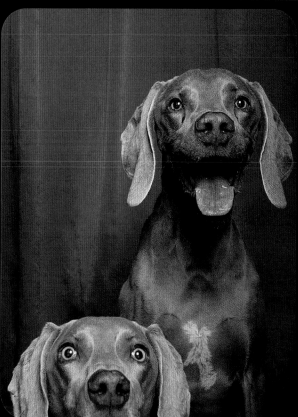

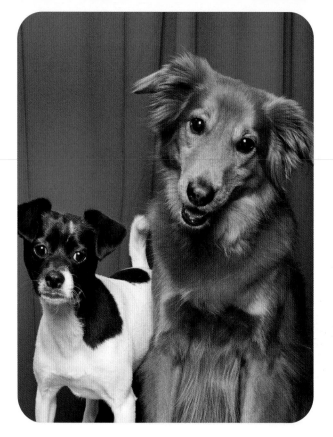
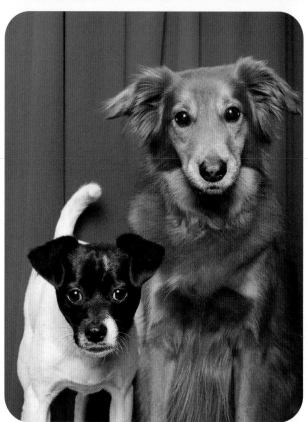
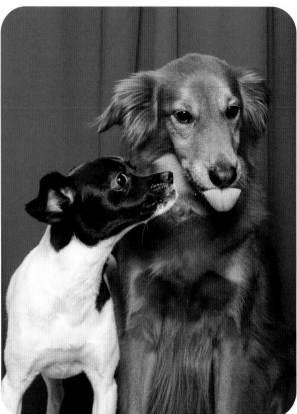
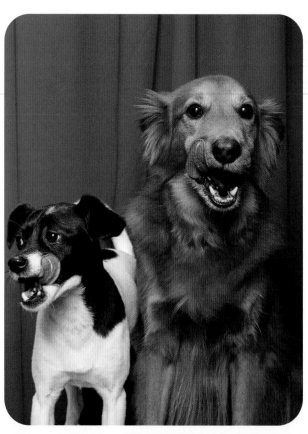

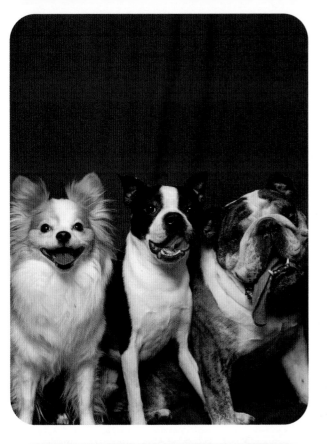
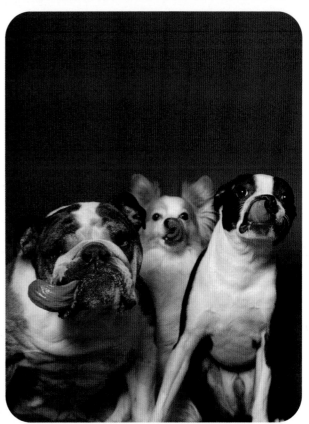
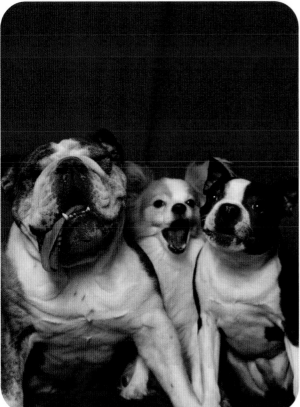
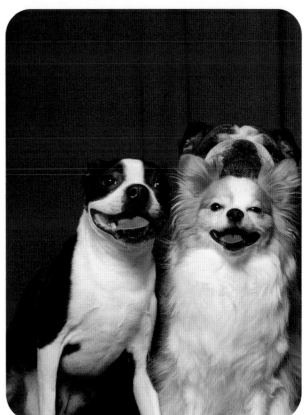

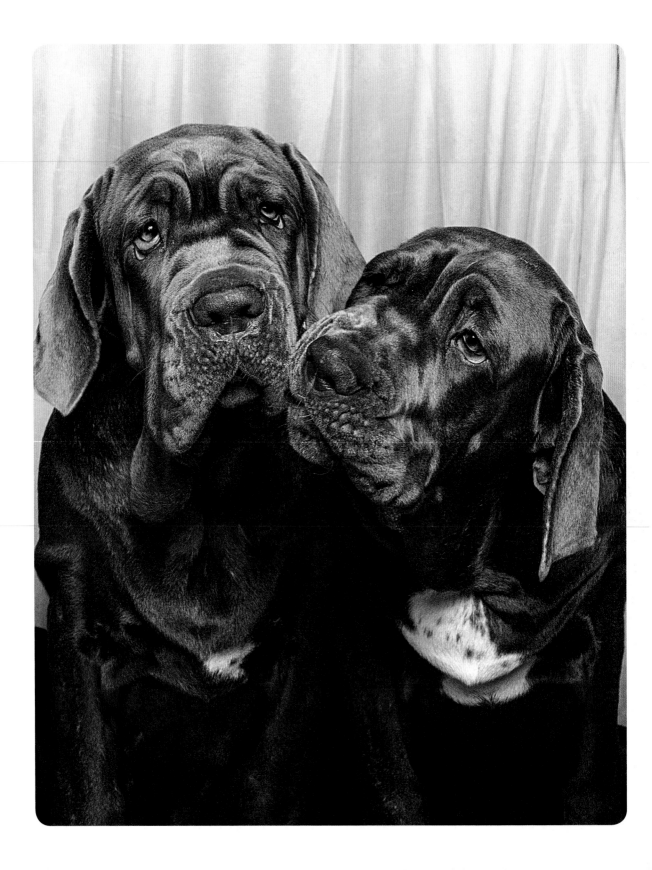

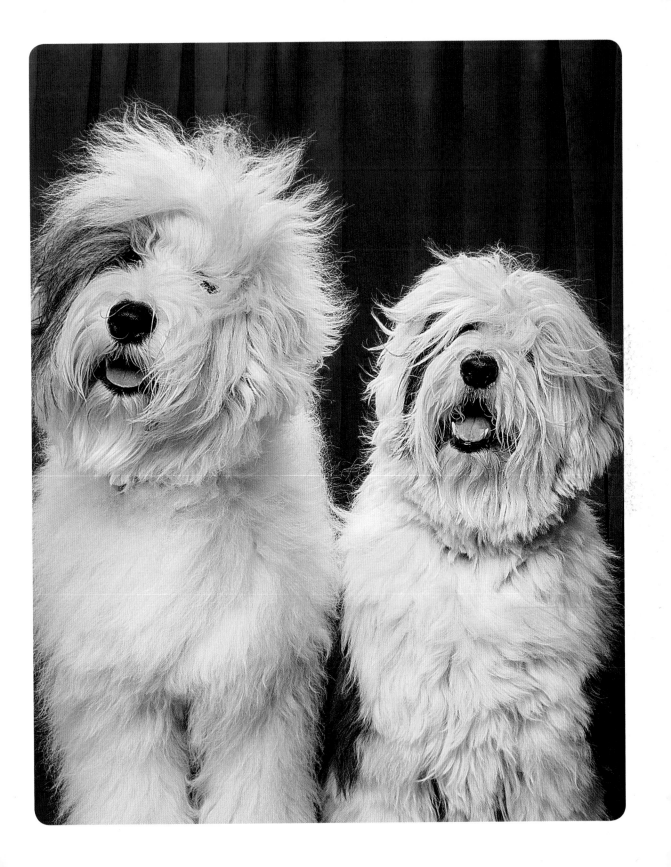

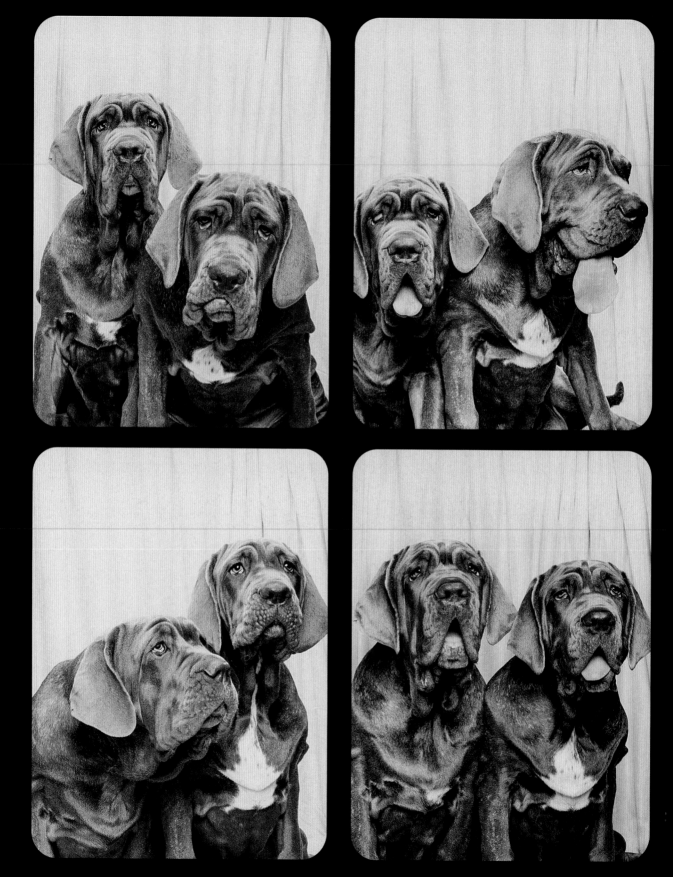

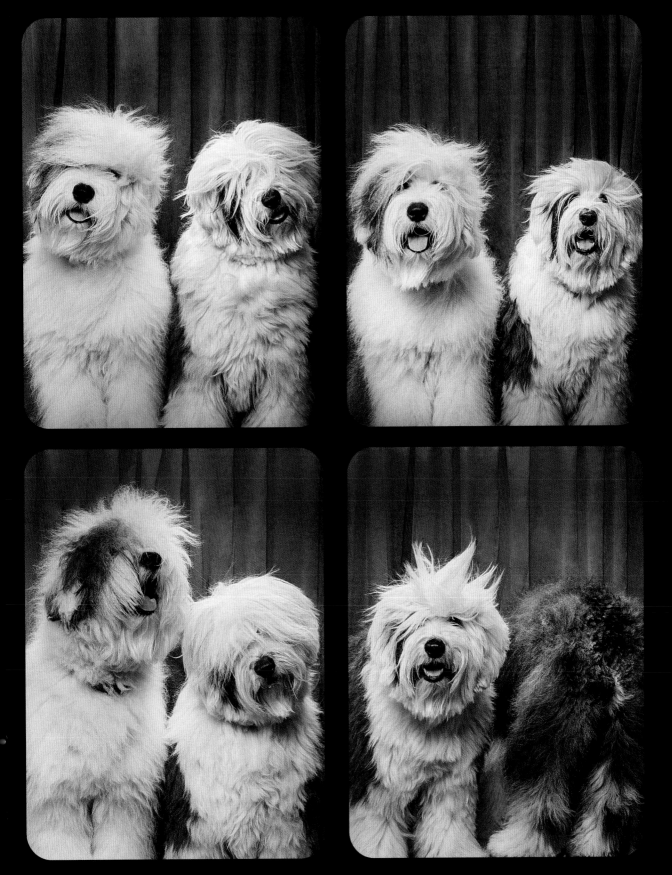

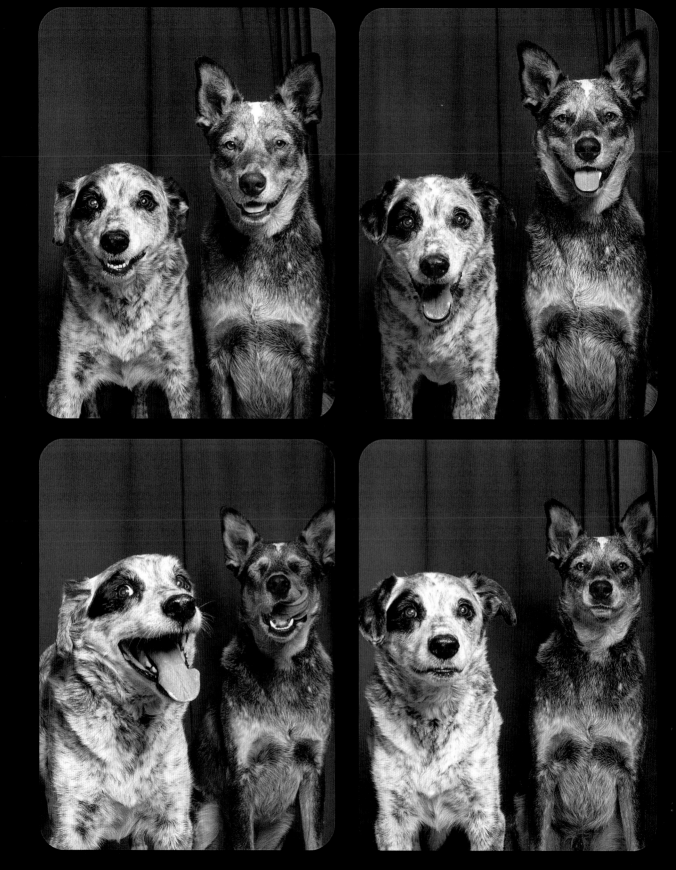

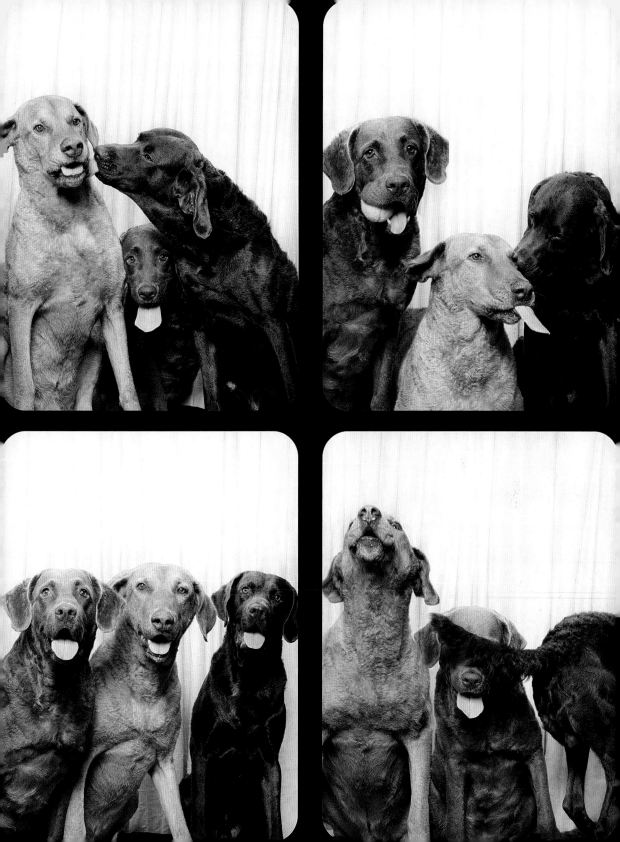

RESCUING DEEDEE

My mother is very allergic to animals, so I didn't grow up with dogs. Or perhaps she just used this as an excuse, because she does love a tidy house. (You know, I've never asked her!) Regardless, she has become very fond of her fur grandbabies over the years.

I was twenty-three when I was introduced to dogs. My boyfriend at the time bought himself a dog under the guise of "a gift for me." I had no idea what to do with a dog, or how to train one. I even said he would be responsible for cleaning up after the dog because the very idea repulsed me. (I had inherited my mother's cleanliness gene.) But then she arrived—a rescue puppy that we named DeeDee—and all bets were off. Cleanliness didn't matter anymore. Fur on the furniture, drool on my clothes, toys everywhere, dog breath in my face. Just like a newborn, she stole my heart with a single look. Immediately upon receiving her, DeeDee became my right-hand girl and the soft spot I had in my heart for animals solidified, and then magnified.

DeeDee was a mixed breed—pit bull and cattle dog was our best guess. DeeDee was not a large dog, and she wasn't aggressive in the least. However, we quickly became victims of the discrimination she received for looking like a pit bull: people crossing the street when we went for walks, mothers pulling their children closer, people asking me, wasn't I scared of what she might do? I had no idea at the time that there was so much animosity toward the breed, and never imagined that it could be reflected onto sweet DeeDee. I had adopted this tiny little puppy that had been neglected by its owner, left in the cold rain, starving and suffering from mange. She was no threat to me or to anyone. She loved going for walks, playing with other dogs, snuggling, and eating. And yet here I was encountering this prejudice. I began reading everything I could about the breed so I could be ready for every debate I encountered. I became so passionate about this subject that I wanted to do anything I could to help these underdogs.

I searched out a local rescue group, Mutts-N-Stuff, where I could volunteer. This particular rescue frequently dealt with pit bull breeds, and they had a great passion and understanding for the breed. Through them, I started fostering dogs, but I didn't last long before adopting one of my fosters. DeeDee needed a companion and this young blue pit came along and stole my heart. He came with some major baggage that would make him harder to adopt, but I was determined. Ten years later, Storm has transformed into an exceptional little man that I love as dearly as I did DeeDee. Over the past eleven years, DeeDee and Storm have lived with at least twenty different dogs I have fostered and rehomed. They also have two cat brothers as permanent fixtures and, as of this year, a new baby to share our home. We have most definitely made up for all the years I never had pets!

When I adopted DeeDee, I was studying photography in college, so she became a test subject, whether she liked it or not. The quality of photography I was producing at the time wasn't worth boasting about, but I was drawn even then to animals as subjects. When I began volunteering with Mutts-N-Stuff it only made sense to bring my camera. I would show up every weekend at their local adoption sites and take pictures of the adoptable pets. Nothing particularly flashy, in my opinion, but apparently it helped get the animals adopted faster. This was back in 2005 and there wasn't a focus on photography of shelter animals like there is now.

Over the years, I have continued to work with Mutts-N-Stuff but have also extended my services to multiple local animal rescues. Through my photography, I have had the opportunity to generate much-needed revenue for these organizations. In return, I have been able to produce a huge collection of beautiful imagery. The rescues I have worked with have always been grateful for what I do, but I am just as grateful to them. I truly believe that I owe my career to animal rescue. Even though my range in photography is more than animals, nothing brings me more joy. Not everyone can love their job. I get to go to work daily and be surrounded by the endless love and amusement animals bring us. I am forever grateful for this path, to which both DeeDee and animal rescue organizations have led me.

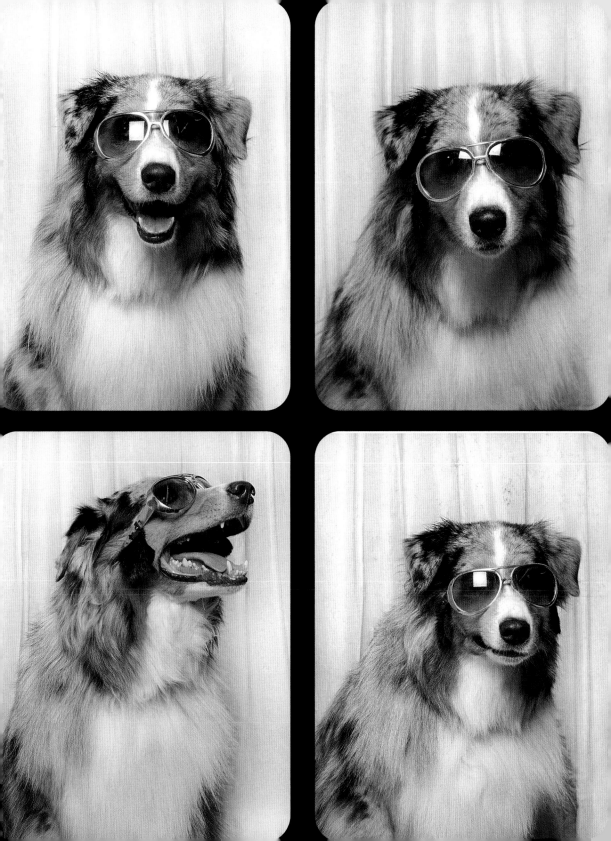

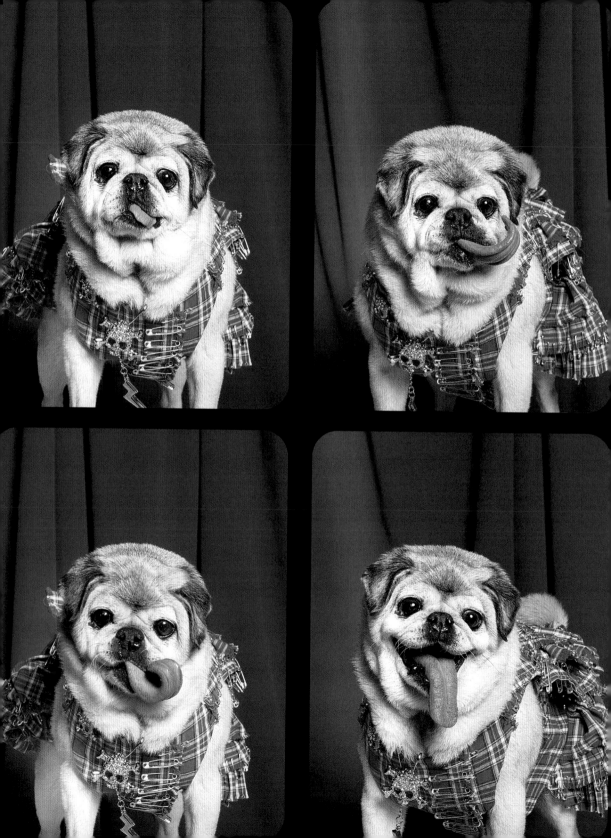

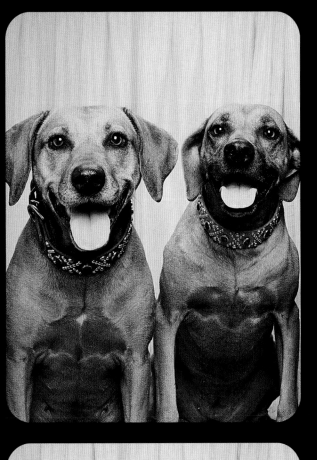
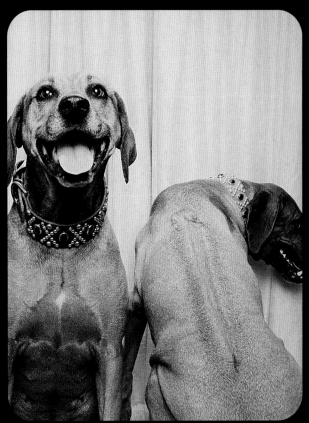
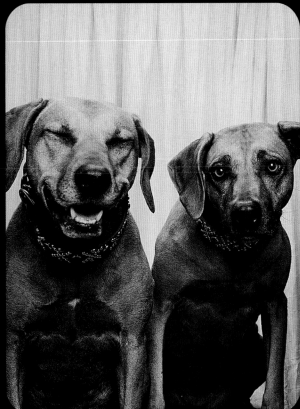
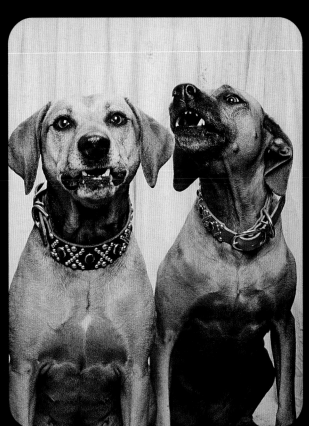

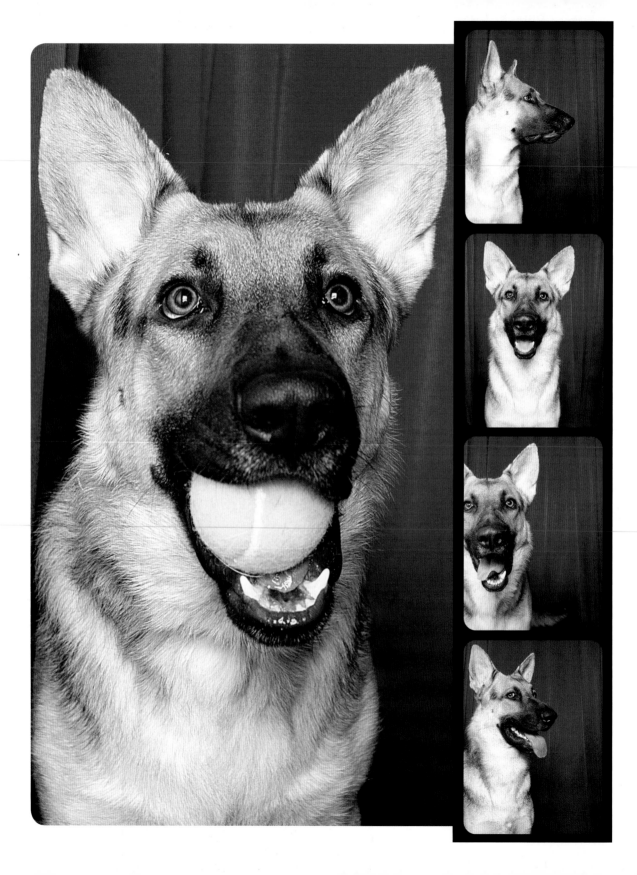

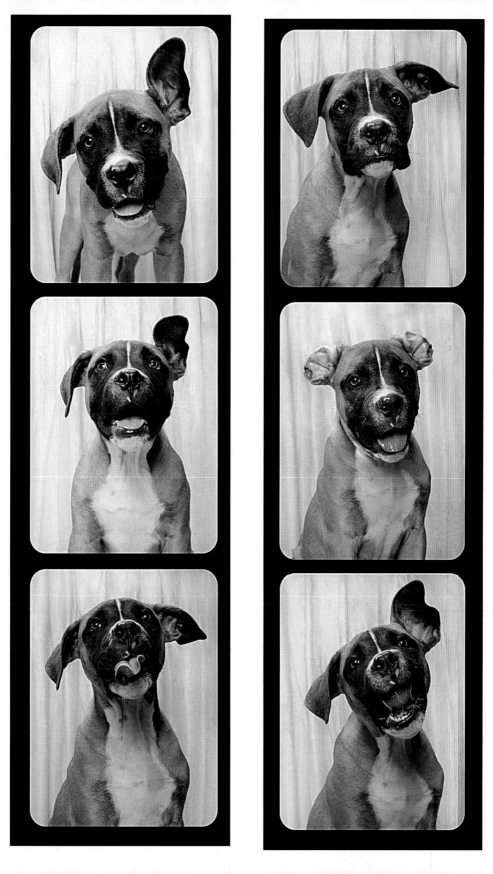

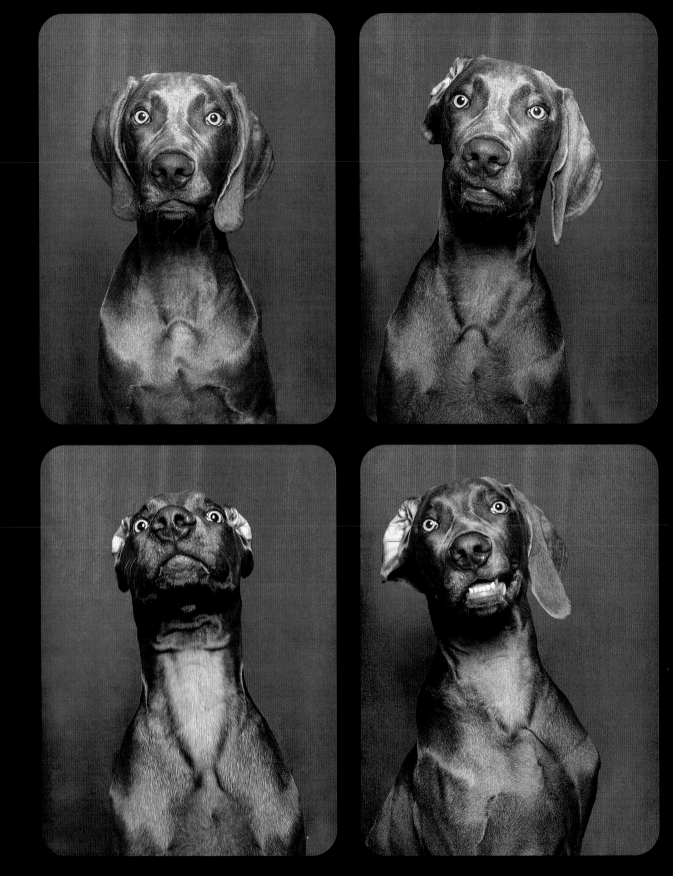

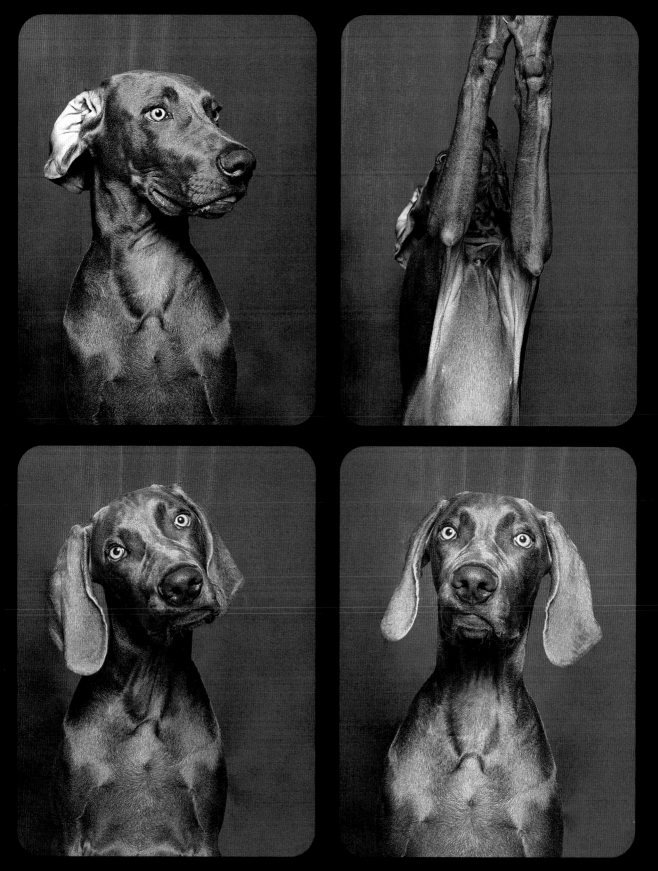

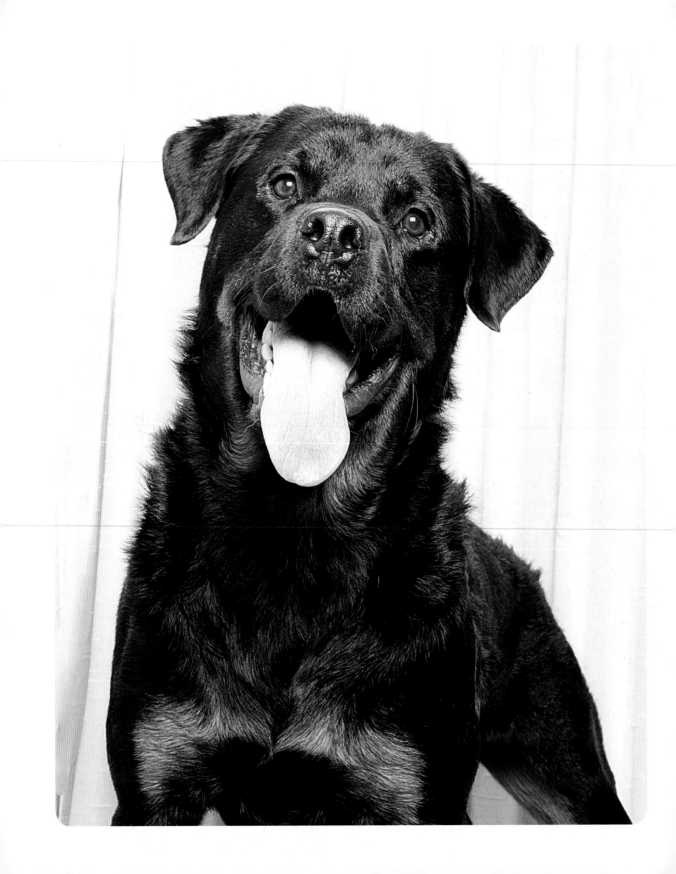

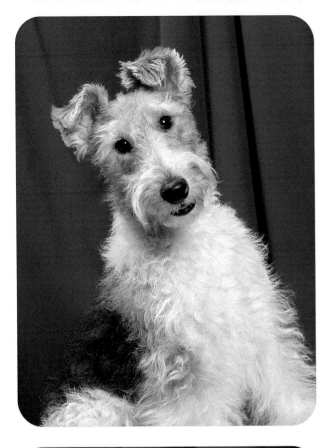
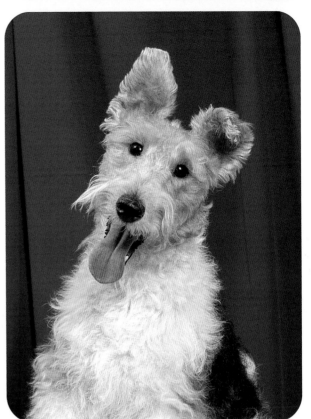
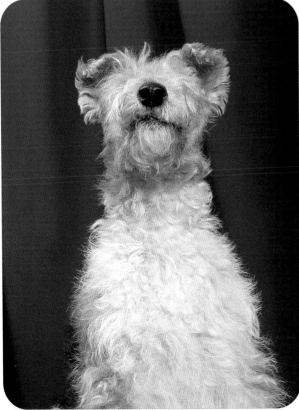
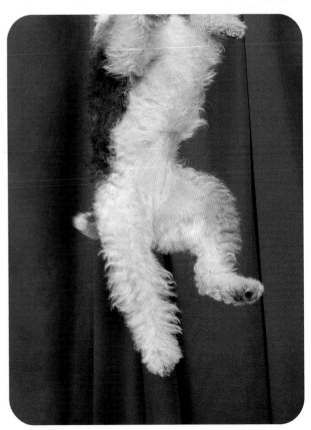

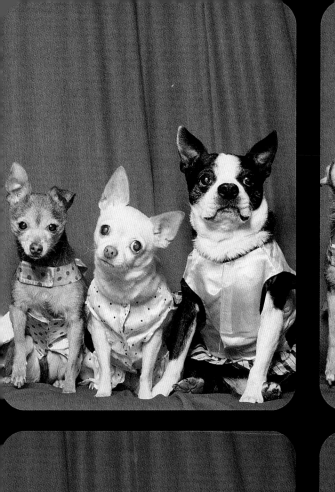
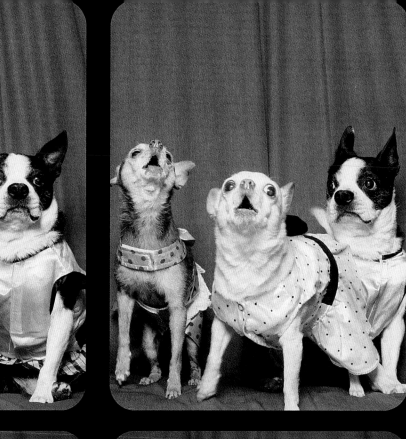
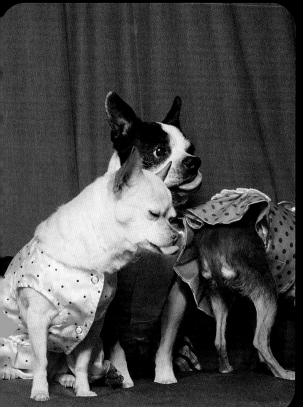
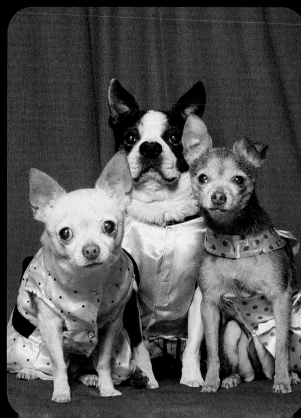

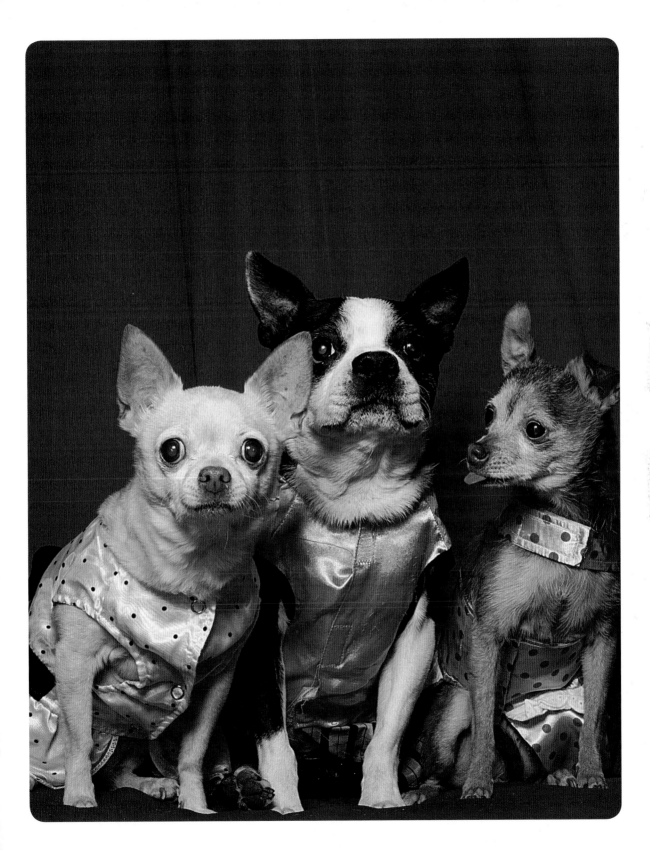

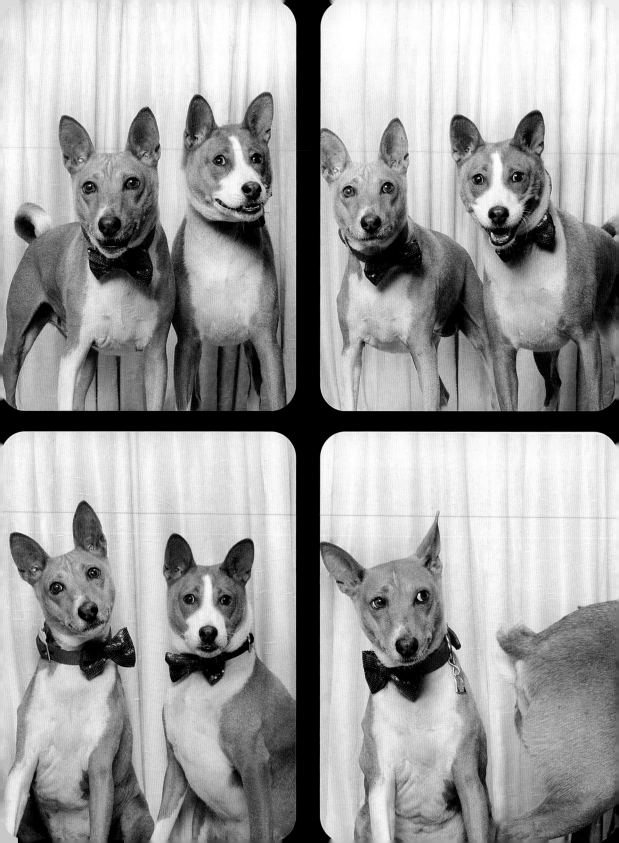

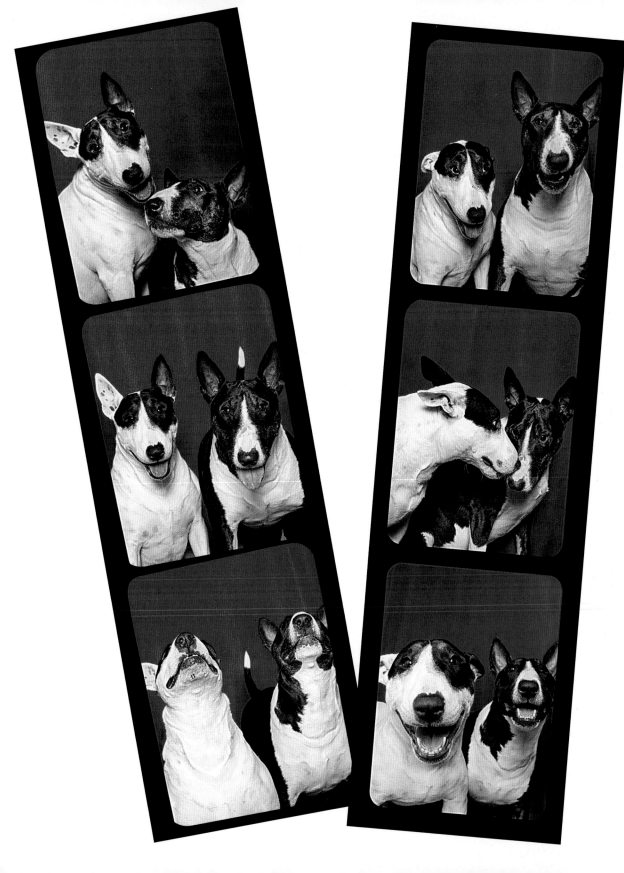

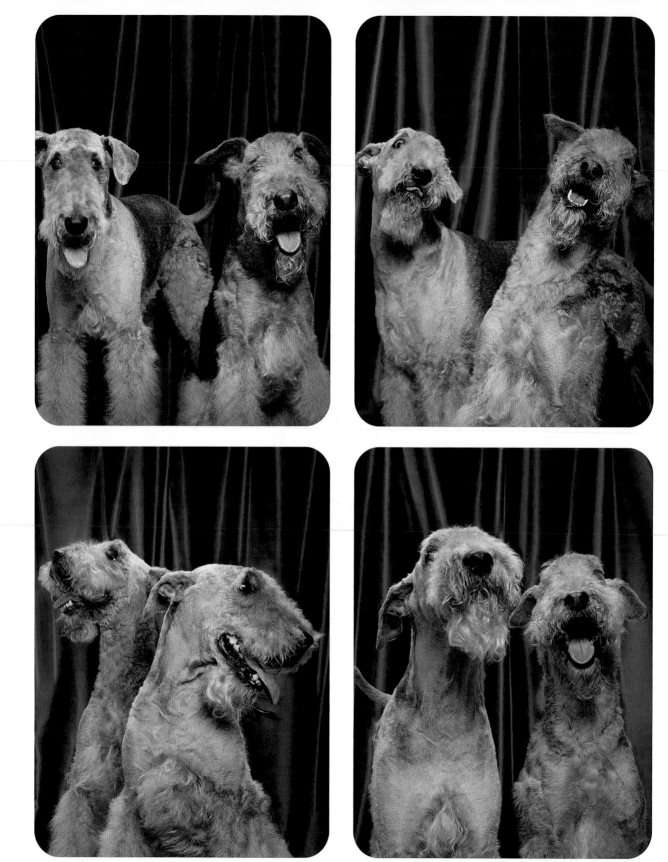

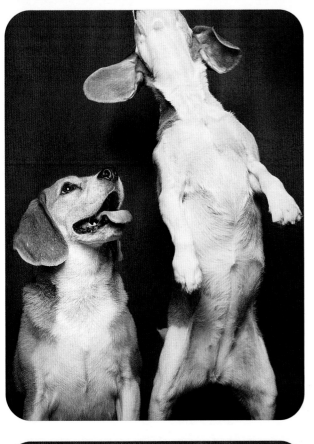
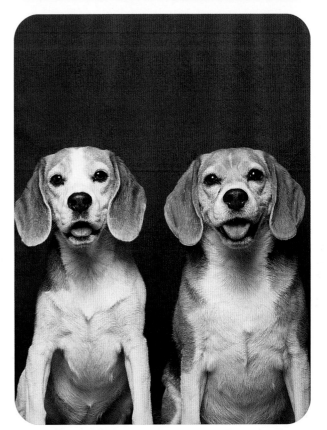
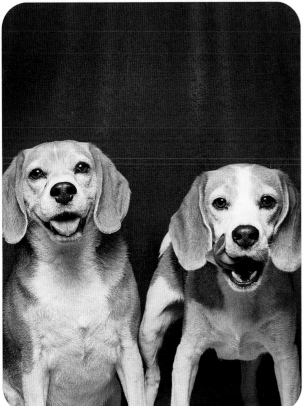
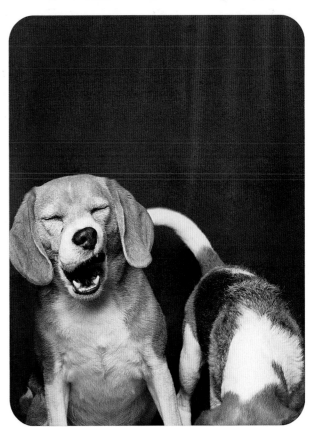

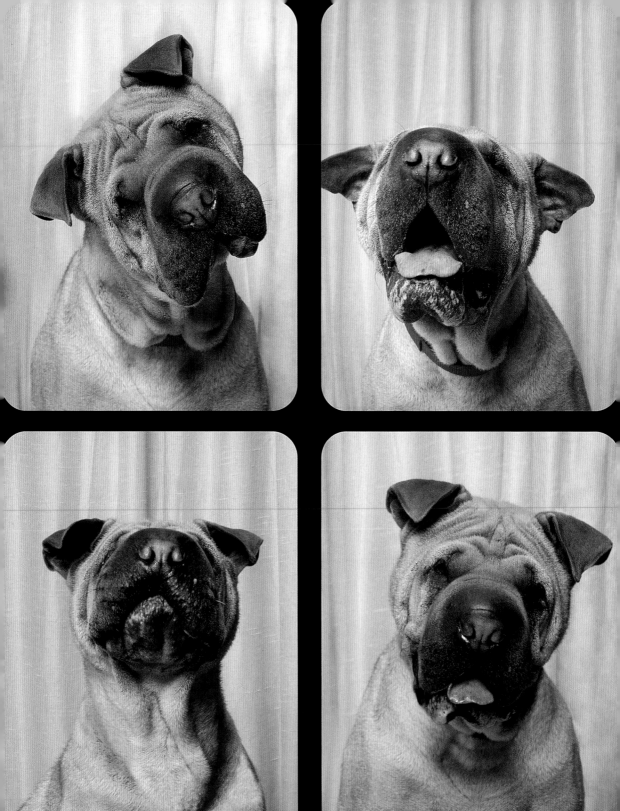

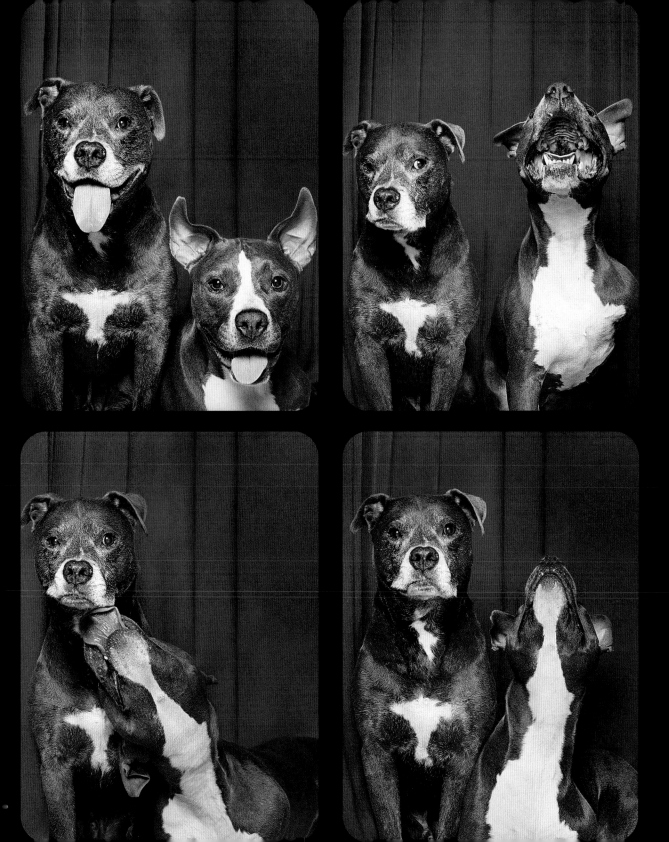

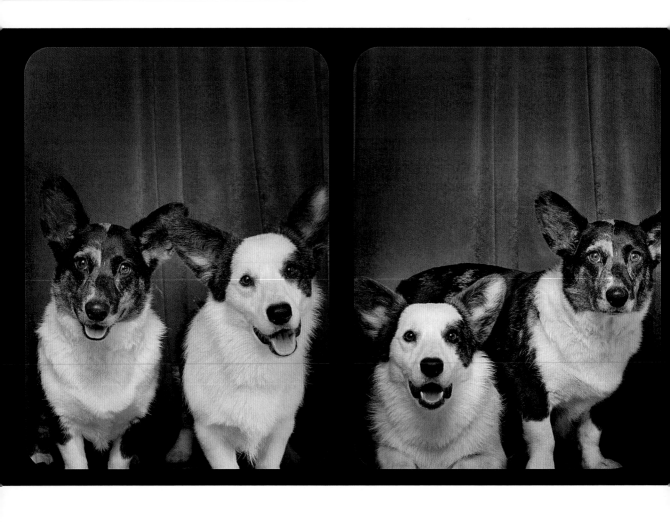

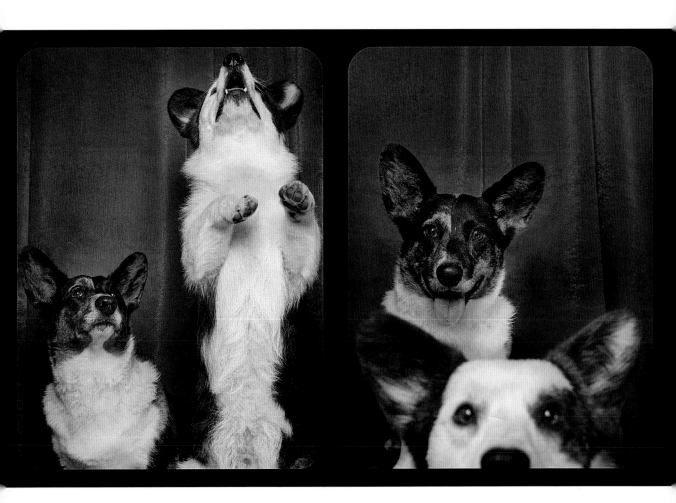

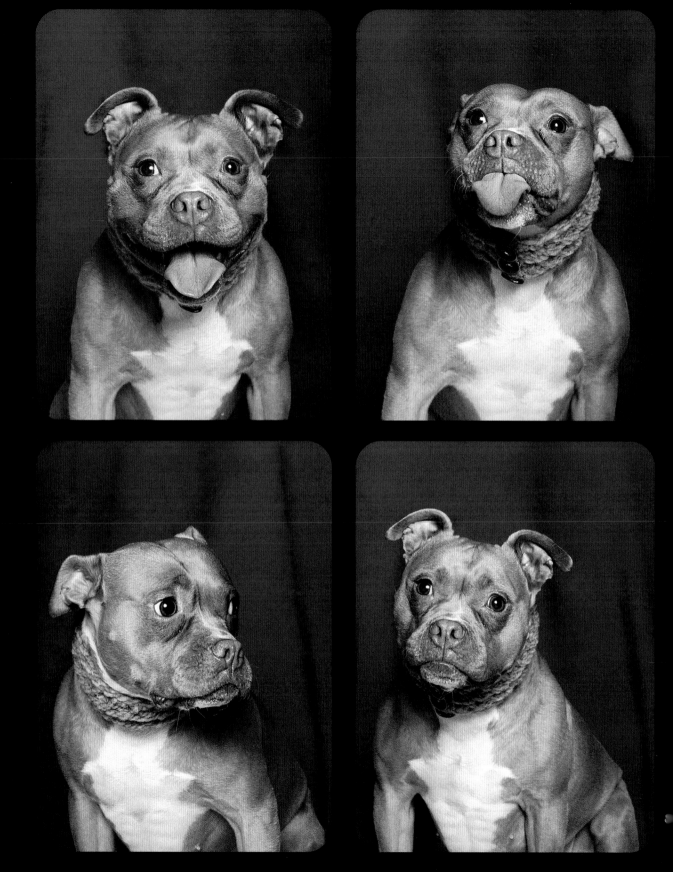

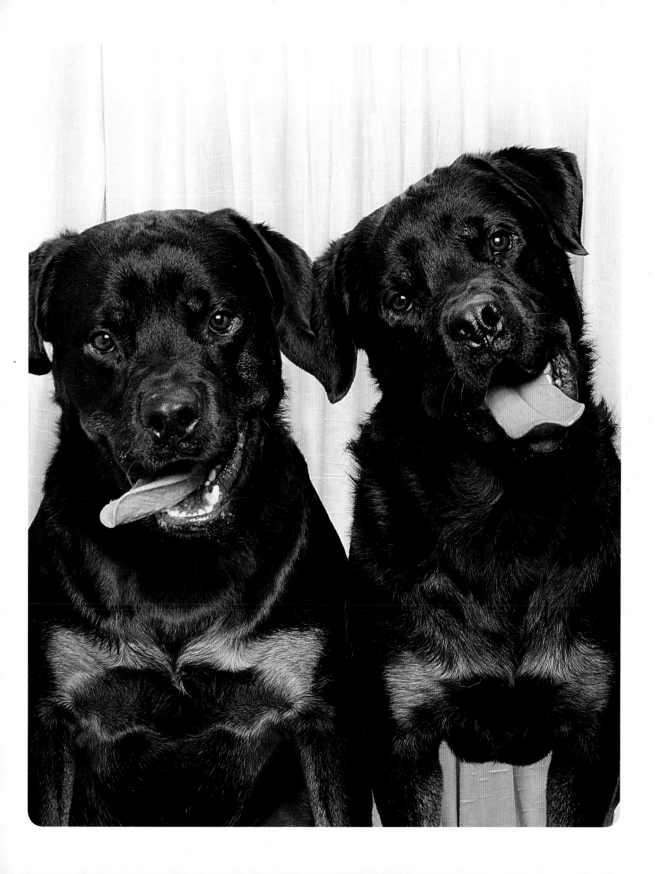

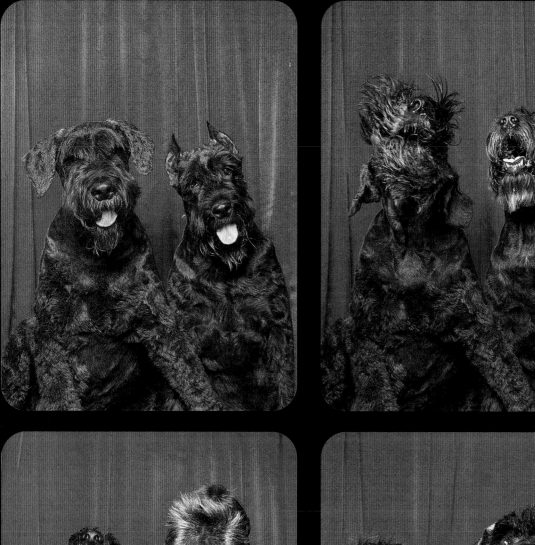
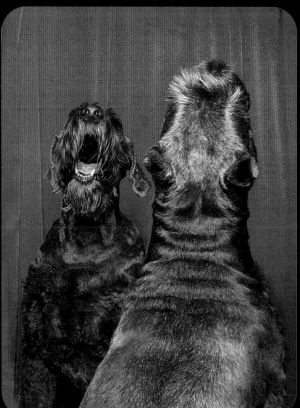
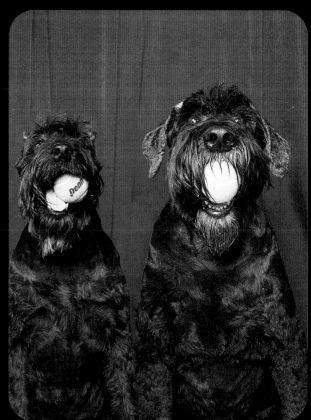

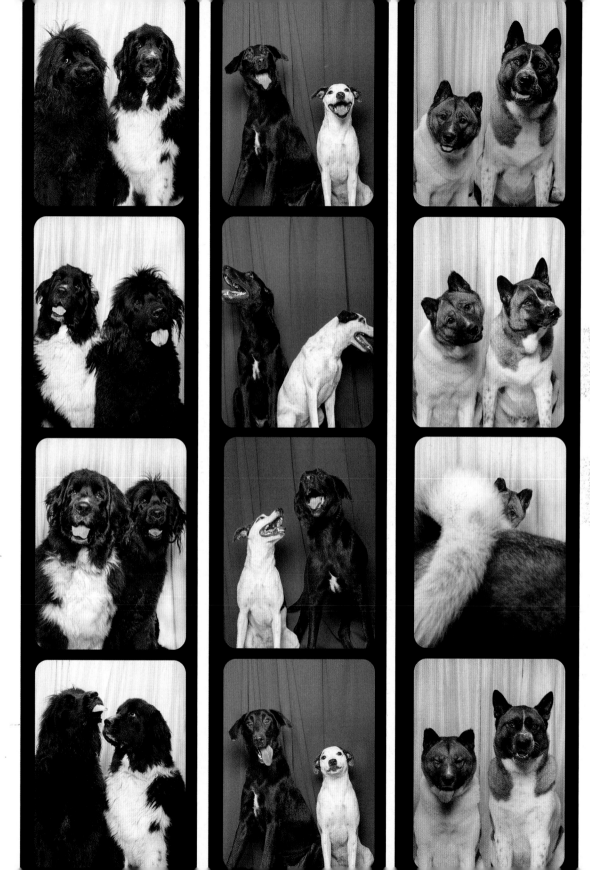

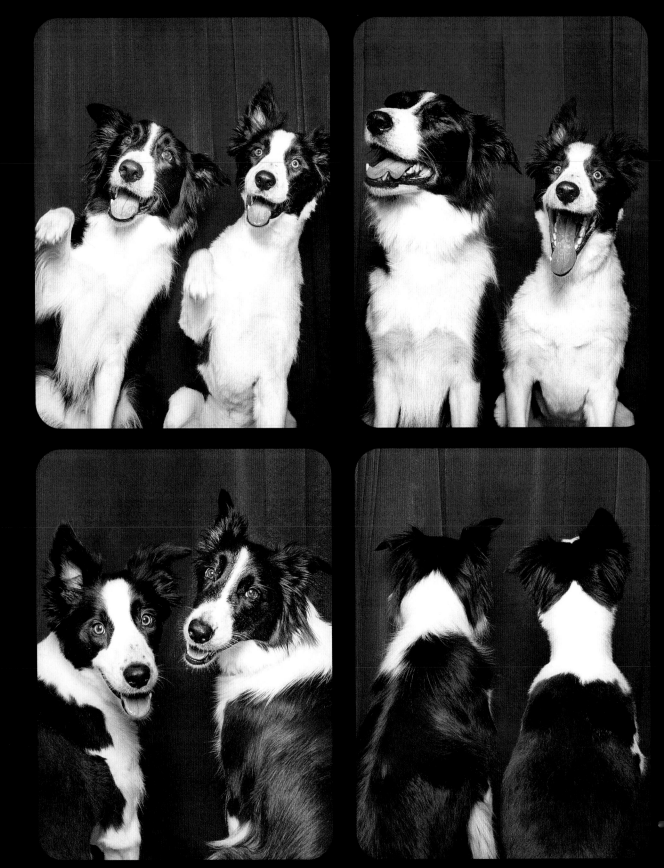

A DAY IN THE LIFE

The one thing everybody asks me when they see my photo booth series is, "How do you get the dogs to *do* that?" Well, I have a few guidelines I follow when it comes to photographing dogs, which I've developed over years of working with all kinds of animals. Typically, when owners arrive at the studio with their dogs, I have them take leashes off the dogs or at least drop the leashes and let the dogs explore. I don't start shooting right away. It's a new environment. They need to scope it out and feel comfortable in the space. Not to mention they tend to get excited or nervous when brought to a new place. They usually need to decompress, and so they get to sniff out all the other smells and run around a little. I must admit there are definitely a few spots in my studio that have been "claimed" by visiting male dogs! The same spots over and over—which leads me to my next rule. Make sure dogs have gone to the bathroom before coming in! Not only to keep my studio cleaner, but because I've found dogs will start acting out on set if they have to go. Since they aren't sure how to communicate "Hey, I need to go outside" to their owners in a new space, it's usually the first reason they get restless on set.

I have an arsenal of treats and noisemakers at the ready when photographing a dog. I have owners bring their own treats if they have dogs with specific diets. Otherwise, I have found a few choice treats that no dog can resist, even if they aren't treat motivated. (Two words: *Peanut. Butter.*) I also have squeakers, duck calls, and even my own voice to get their attention. In fact, my voice is my signature trait and my lethal weapon. Some dogs don't respond to a squeaker toy, but they may get inquisitive when they hear a low grumble or a very high-pitched sound. I have found myself making some of the weirdest noises I didn't even know I could make to get their attention. It may annoy every person in the room, but 90 percent of the time, it'll stop a dog in its tracks and get me a great photo.

Over the years, photographing so many dogs and having so many dogs pass through my home has actually helped teach me a great deal about dog behavior. It's made taking photos easier, especially when I'm dealing with an untrained dog, or a nervous dog, or a dog that's smarter than everyone on the shoot. I can use their nonverbal cues to figure out what I need to do to execute the shots. Overall, I've found that the dogs I photograph fall into three basic categories:

🐾 Well-disciplined

With the well-disciplined dogs, the photo shoot is usually a no-brainer. As long as they can do a sit-stay, I can get every kind of shot I imagined. Although I do get thrown a curve ball on occasion when the dog is so well behaved that it literally sits and stays and has only one look. Then I have to get extra inventive to get the shot.

🐾 Totally balls-to-the-wall high energy

The insanely high energy dog usually takes a bit more patience. You aren't going to get the shot right away. The first round of images is probably going to be a blur of fur. Most people leaving these shoots comment on how hard my job is—it can be sweaty, and there's a lot of jumping around and wrangling excited canine subjects. It does take a lot more time and patience than I think people estimate. So does train-ing your dog—and that's essentially what we're doing. By the end, the dogs either get the hang of it or they've grown bored with us and tend to settle into the role anyway.

These dogs are also great at giving you what you want when every-one in the room ignores them. Sit the owner down and engage him in conversation. It's amusing what happens next—suddenly the dog that had no time for posing pulls out every trick in the book!

🐾 Completely scared

Some dogs may have come from a bad past or aren't used to new environments. With a genuinely frightened dog, I don't start shooting right away. We just hang out and pet the dog. Once we are on set, I start rewarding them right away. Treats aren't usually of interest to a nervous dog, so most of the time I keep it quiet on set, keeping the energy really calm and continually reassuring and petting the dog. They need to know it's fun and that nothing bad is happening. If the dog gets anxious, we give her a break. It's important not to rush these shoots.

I also try not to greet the dogs when they first arrive either. It's hard not to go rushing at these cute faces and start hugging and petting them—but I certainly don't like my head being rubbed by a stranger. Why should they? I don't make a lot of eye contact and I sit down at their level and let them come to me. I don't want them to feel threatened by me and I know that trust is necessary on set.

I actually found shooting with the booth much harder than regular shoots. Even though the lighting is more primitive than most of my studio shoots and it looks easy enough to grab four funny shots, the opposite was true. Getting two untrained dogs to not only sit in the confines of a booth but also sit close to each other doesn't always come easy. There are many outtakes, many breaks for the dogs between shots, and a lot of coaxing with treats, noises, and multiple people surrounding the set to keep them from bounding out of the booth. Most of the time it's a game of patience for them to finally figure out what's happening and get comfortable with the situation. Once they know nothing bad is going to happen to them in this boxed area, and once they clue in to all the treats they are receiving for hanging out there, they usually come around.

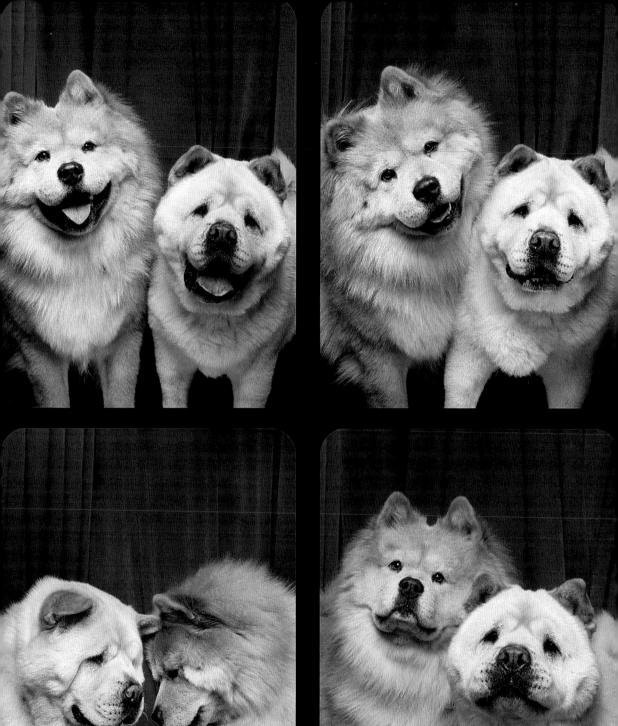

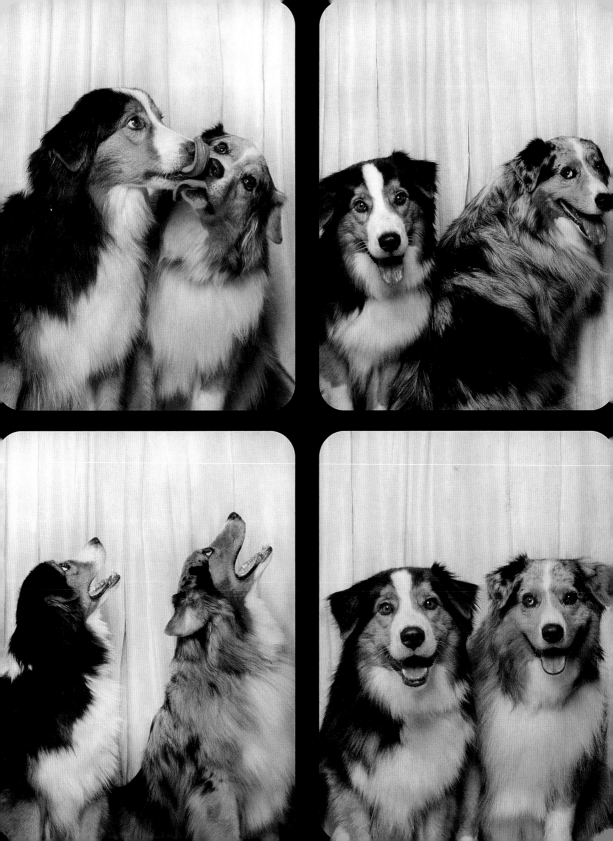

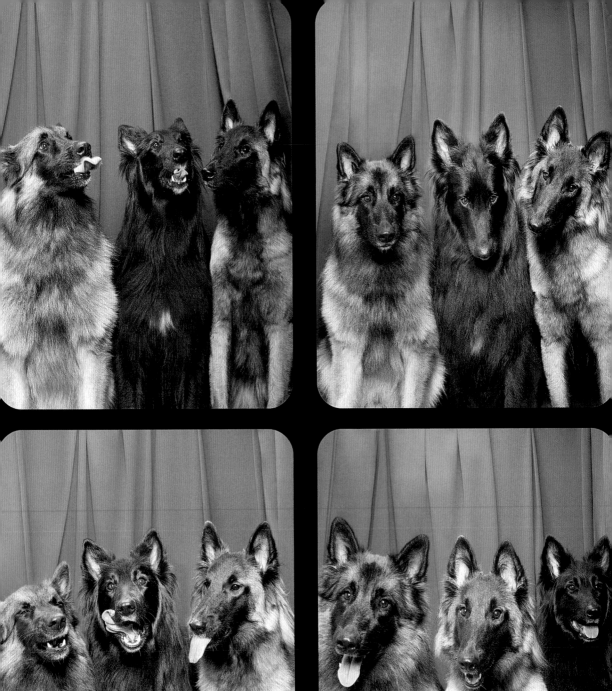

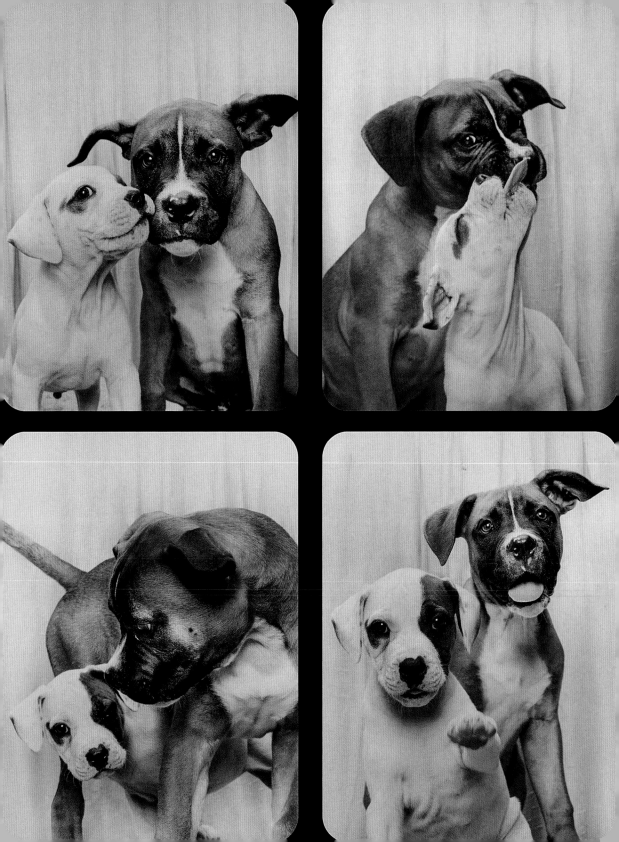

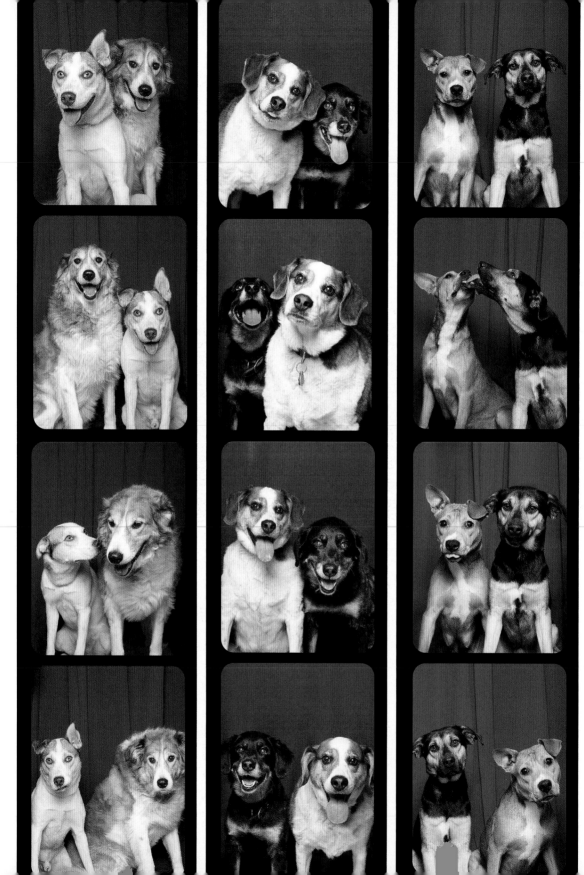

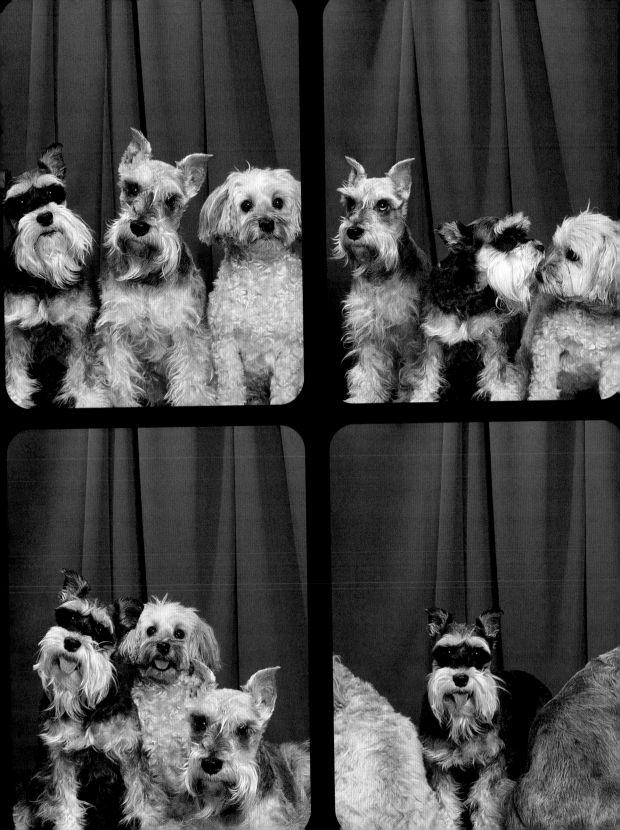

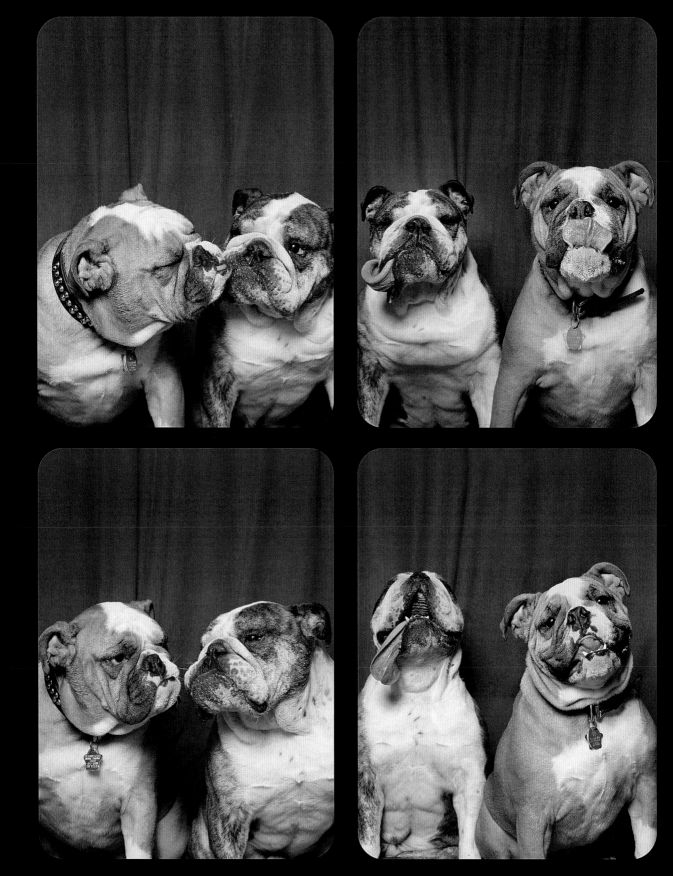

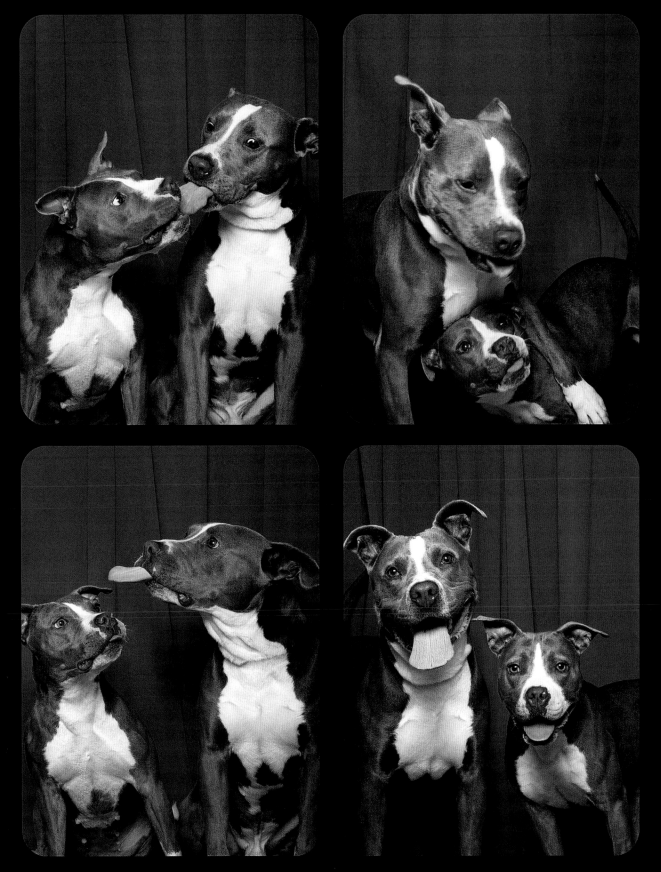

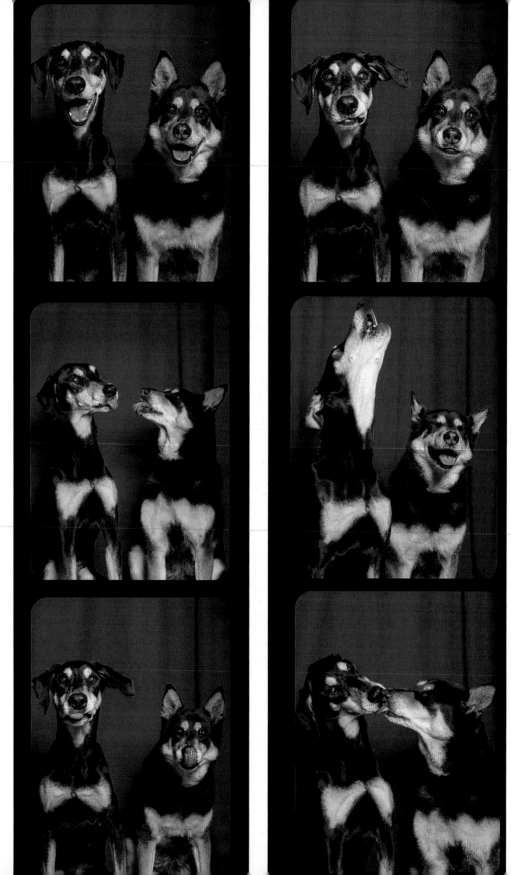

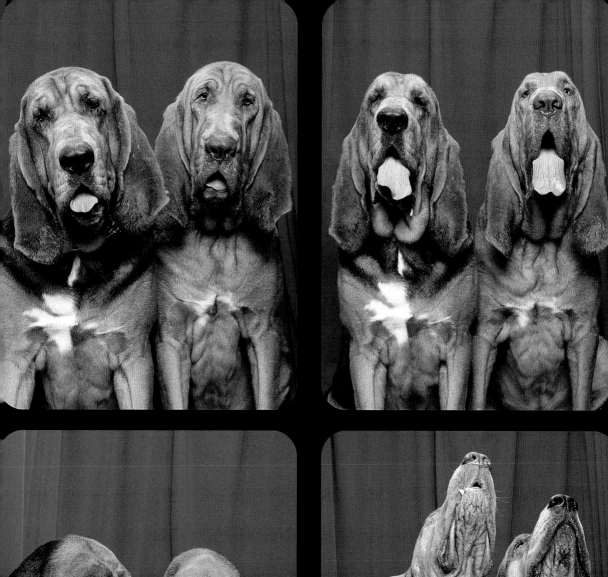
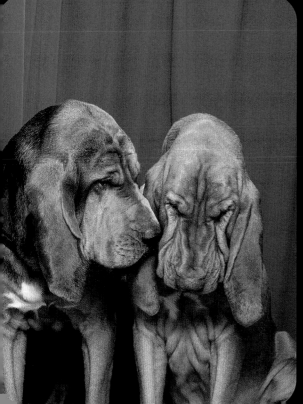
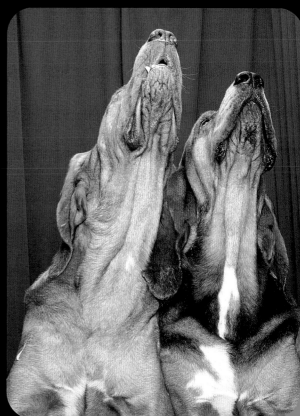

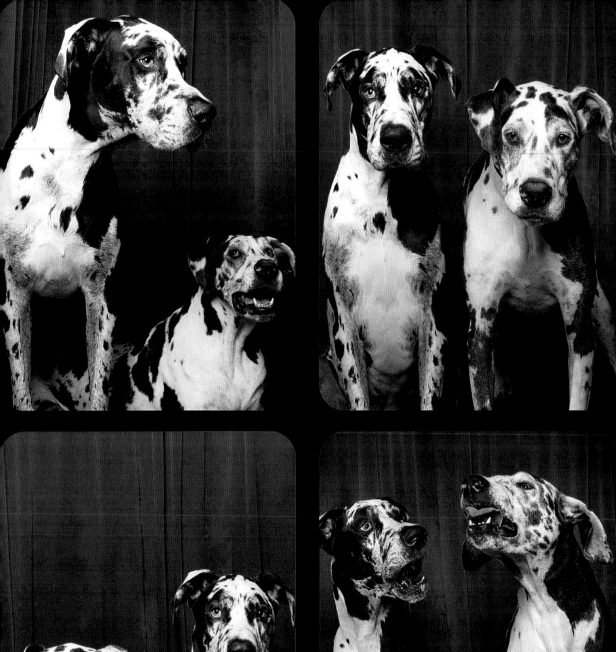
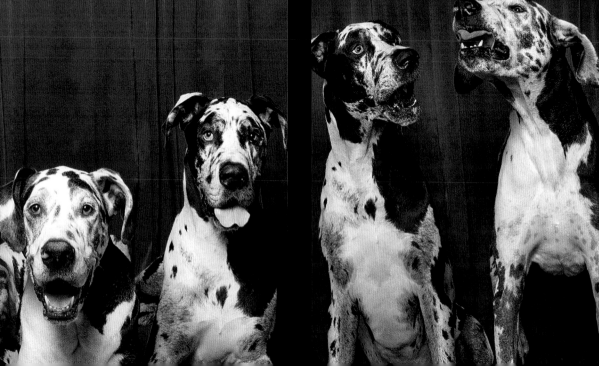

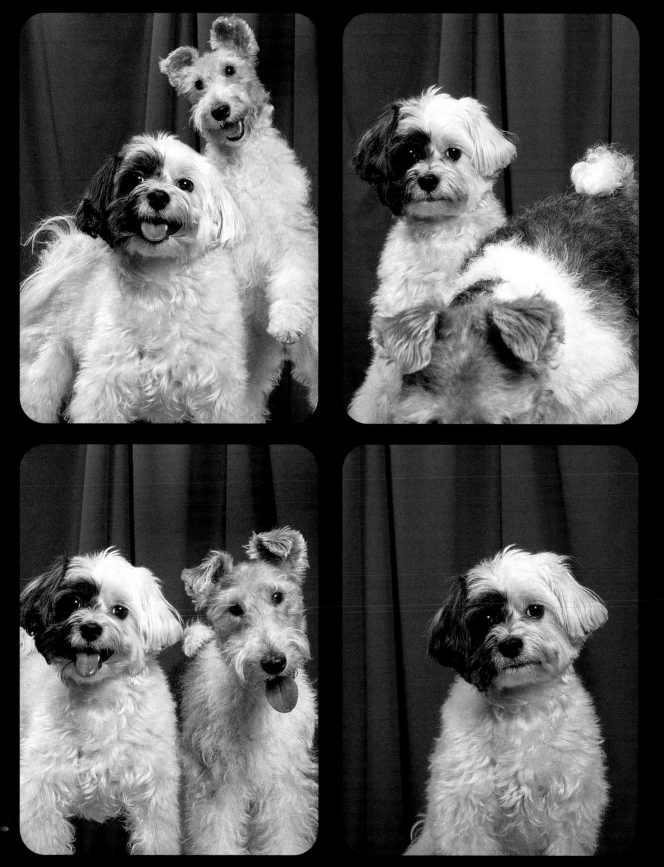

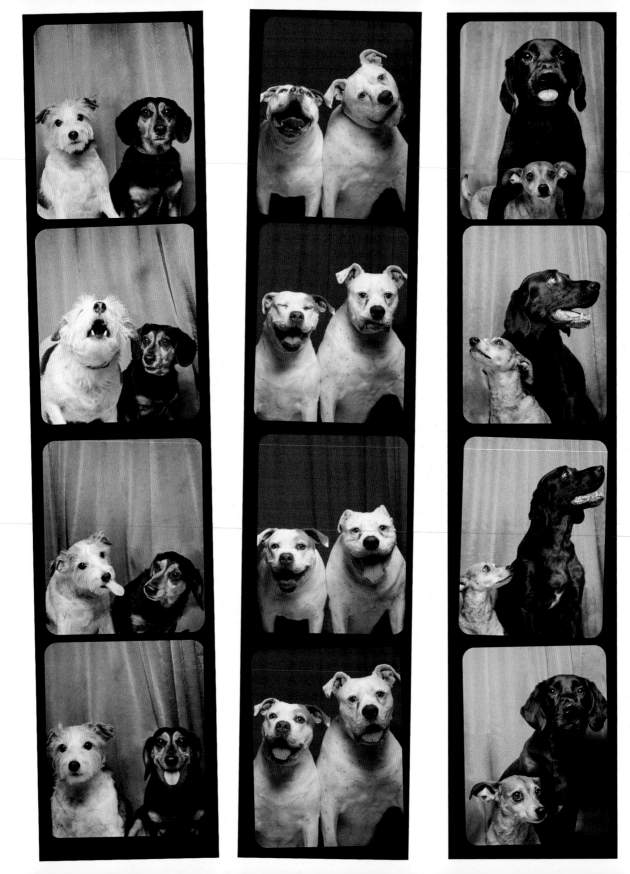

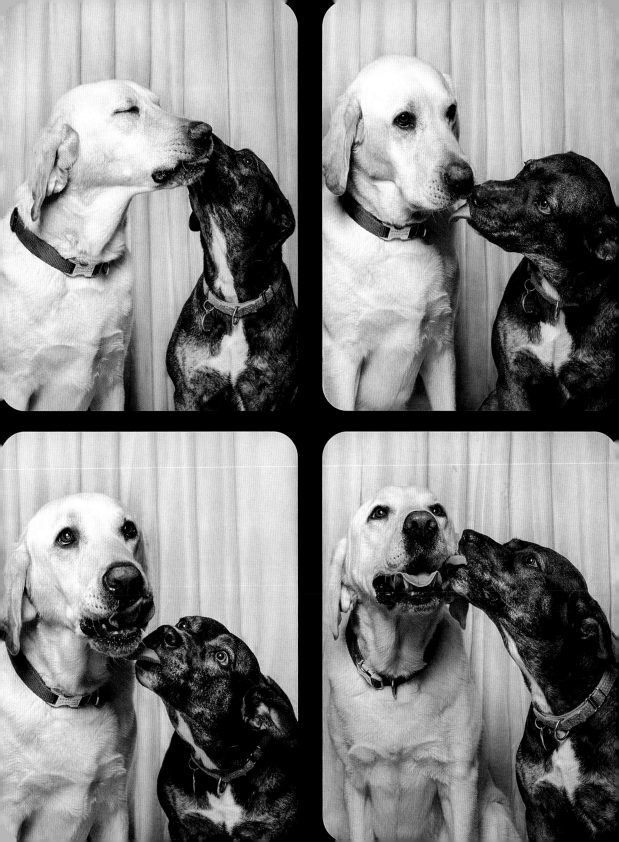

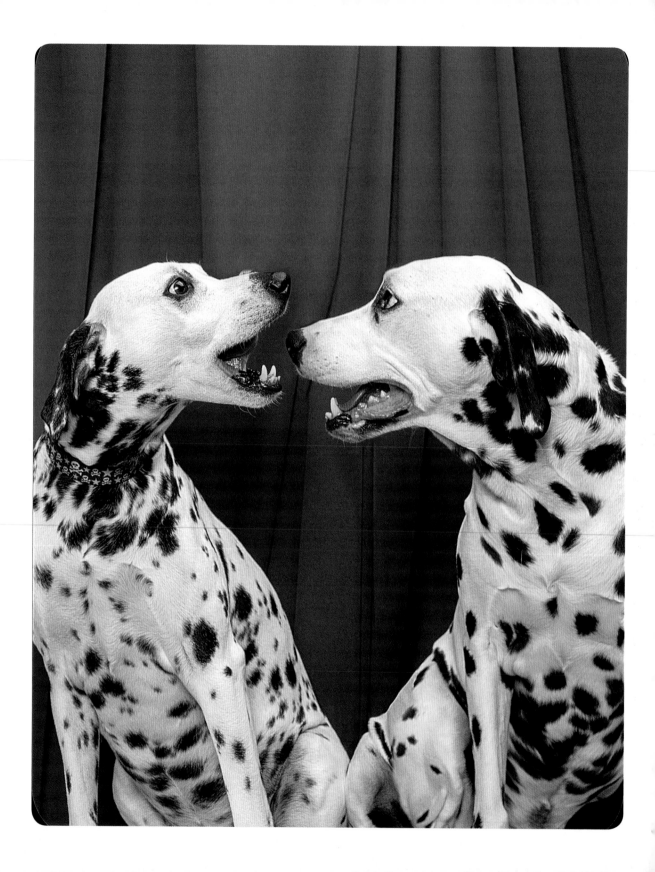

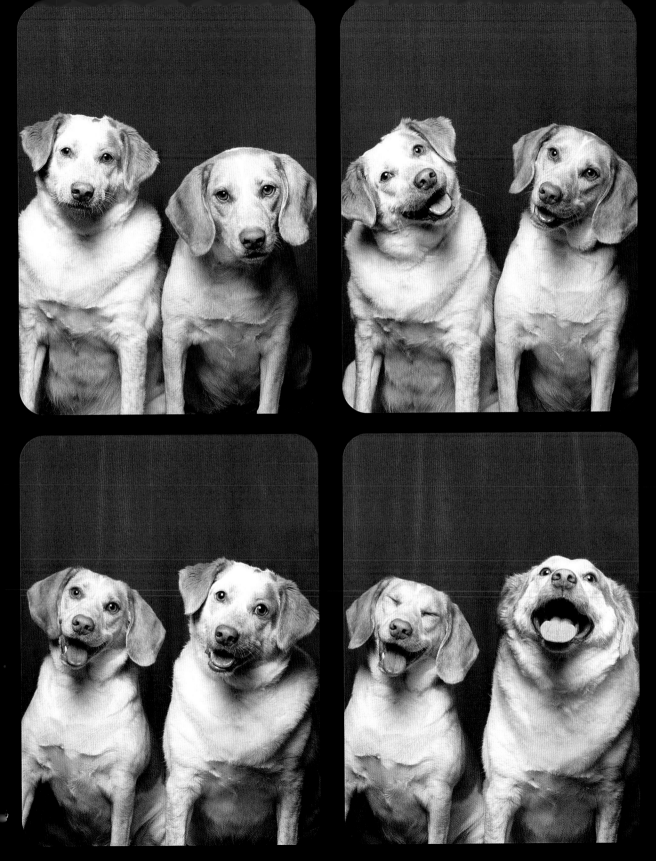

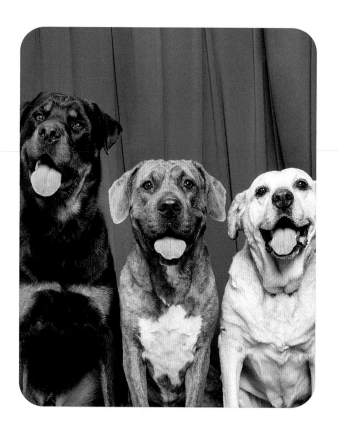
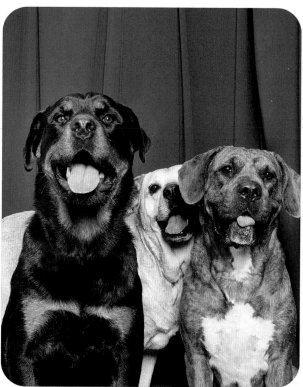
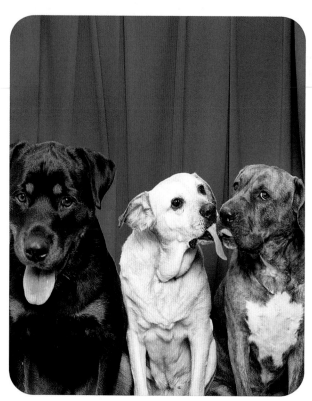
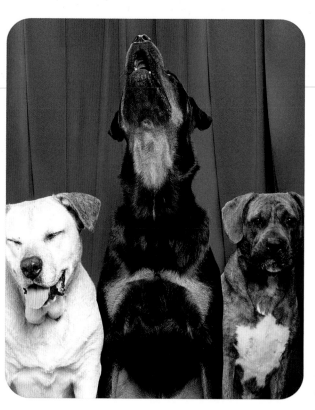

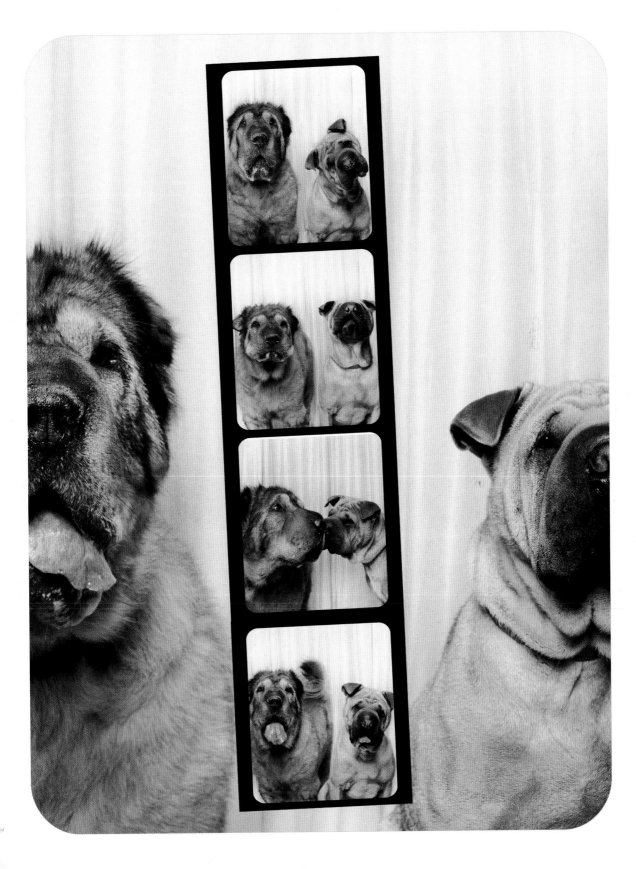

MAN'S (AND WOMAN'S!) BEST FRIEND

DeeDee was with me for fifteen years. That's longer than any job I have had, any home I have lived in, and every relationship. And through all of it, she loved me unconditionally. She was there to support me through both the good and the bad. When I was bawling my eyes out, I could count on her to simply lean in, snuggle up to me, and lick my tears away. No matter how low I got, she could always make me laugh. She taught me how to love and her devotion made me a better person.

When I was trying to complete my thoughts for this book, I asked friends what their dogs meant to them. The best answer I got was, "We have an old mutt that has very few teeth, bad breath, is scared of his own shadow, and has periodic seizures. I wouldn't trade him for any other dog in the world." Pet owners universally share the same basic answer: nobody can give us the unbridled joy, the unconditional love and warmth our pets give us. In return, we look beyond the fur and floppy ears and wet noses to the real "person" underneath.

With these thoughts, I created this book. I feel these photos resonate for the same reason that dogs and people have been intertwined since the dawn of civilization: dogs love us and want to be with us so much that they reflect our own selves back at us. And when dogs are so willing to show us raw love and happiness, it makes us want to deserve it of them.

If you look through these pages and see, in the unguarded moments, not just a bunch of quirky, adorable dogs, but emotions that you might have thought were only human—love, friendship, annoyance, laughter, confusion, and joy—well, you're the right reader for this book. Fido! Enjoy.

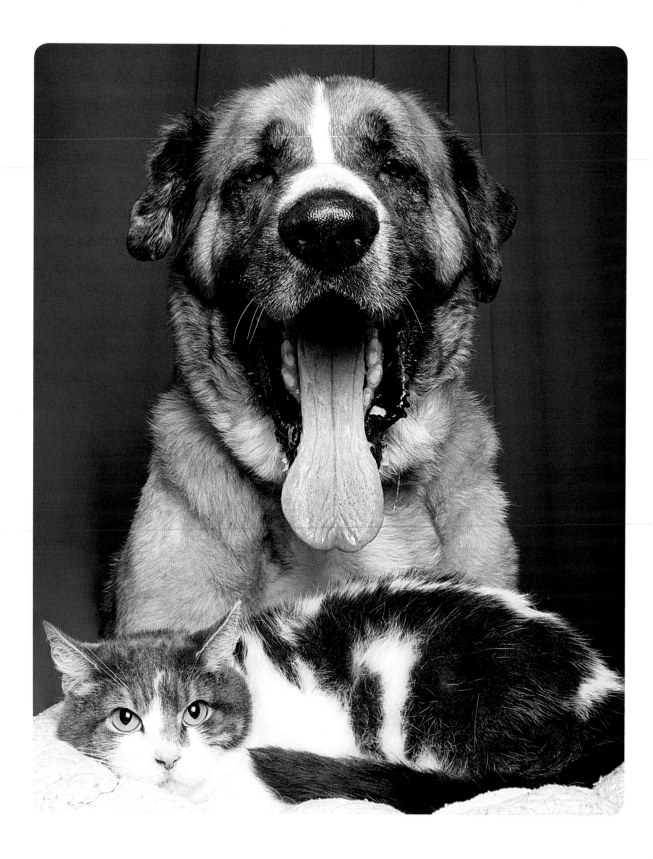

ACKNOWLEDGMENTS

IN ORDER OF APPEARANCE

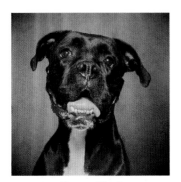

Samerkhet

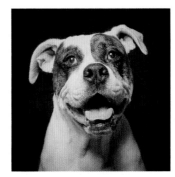

Foxy Brown

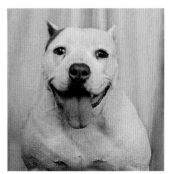

Miss Pitunia

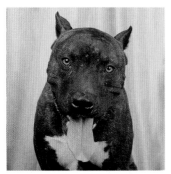

Tucker

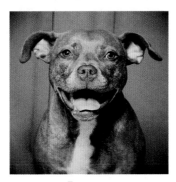

Bumper

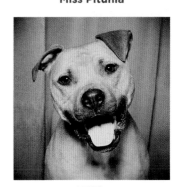

Willis

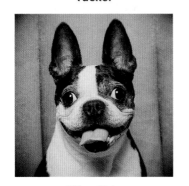

Riley Kate

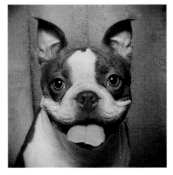

Ronan Dex

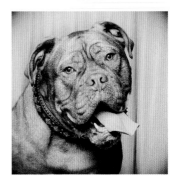

Max

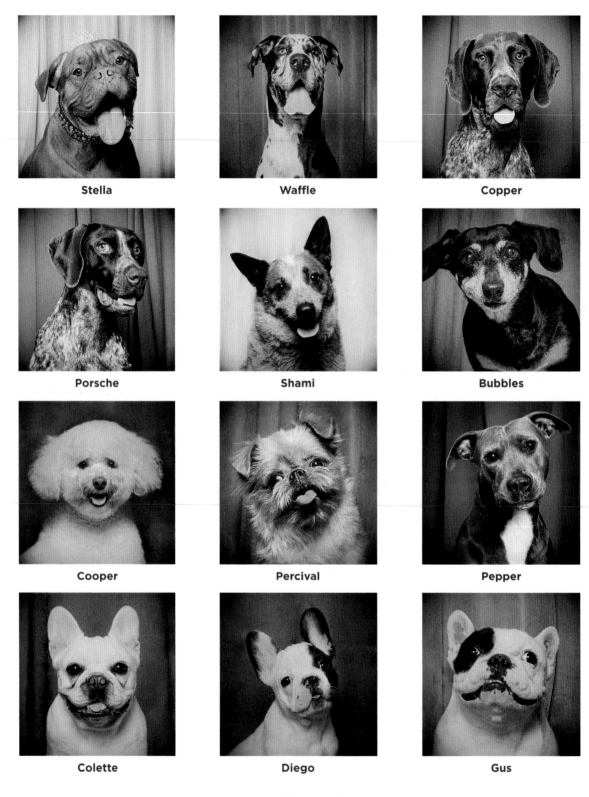

Stella

Waffle

Copper

Porsche

Shami

Bubbles

Cooper

Percival

Pepper

Colette

Diego

Gus

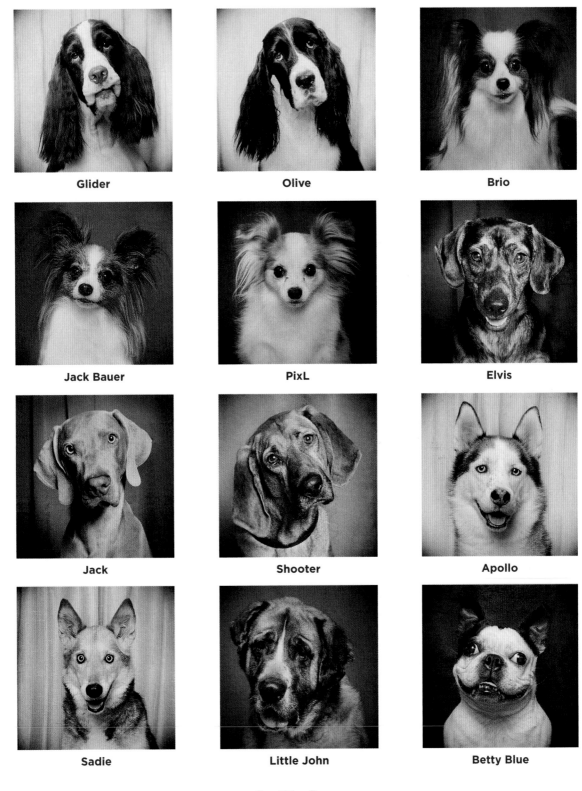

Glider

Olive

Brio

Jack Bauer

PixL

Elvis

Jack

Shooter

Apollo

Sadie

Little John

Betty Blue

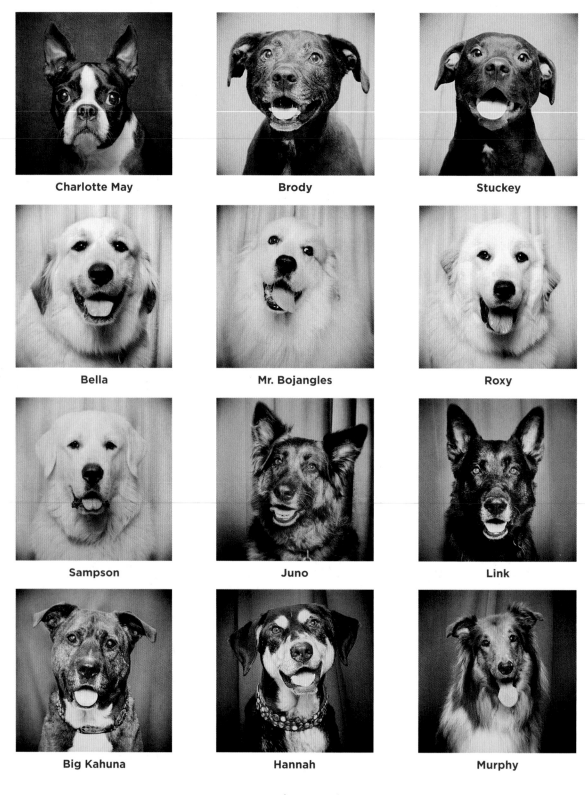

Charlotte May

Brody

Stuckey

Bella

Mr. Bojangles

Roxy

Sampson

Juno

Link

Big Kahuna

Hannah

Murphy

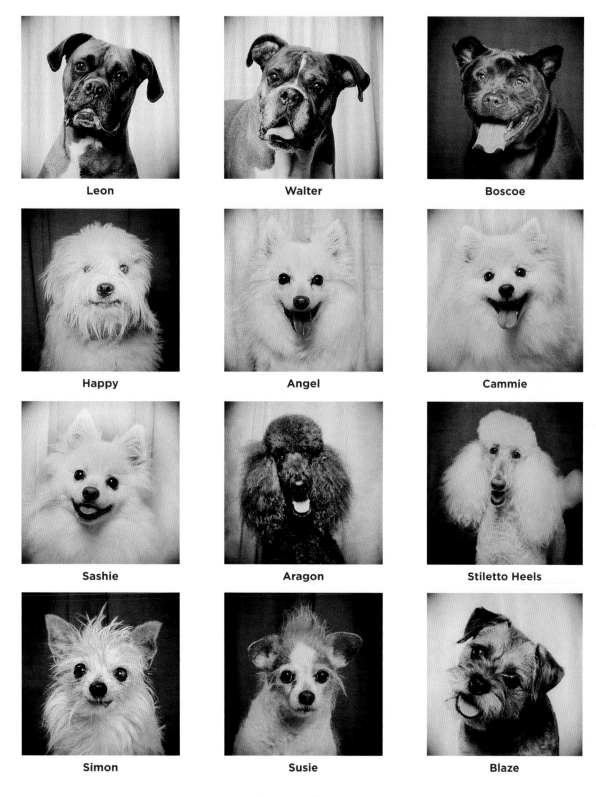

Leon

Walter

Boscoe

Happy

Angel

Cammie

Sashie

Aragon

Stiletto Heels

Simon

Susie

Blaze

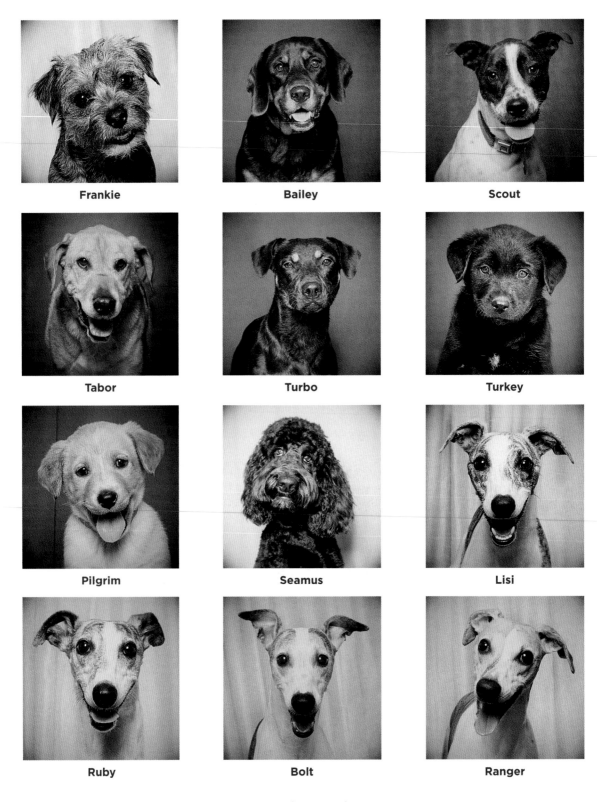

Frankie

Bailey

Scout

Tabor

Turbo

Turkey

Pilgrim

Seamus

Lisi

Ruby

Bolt

Ranger

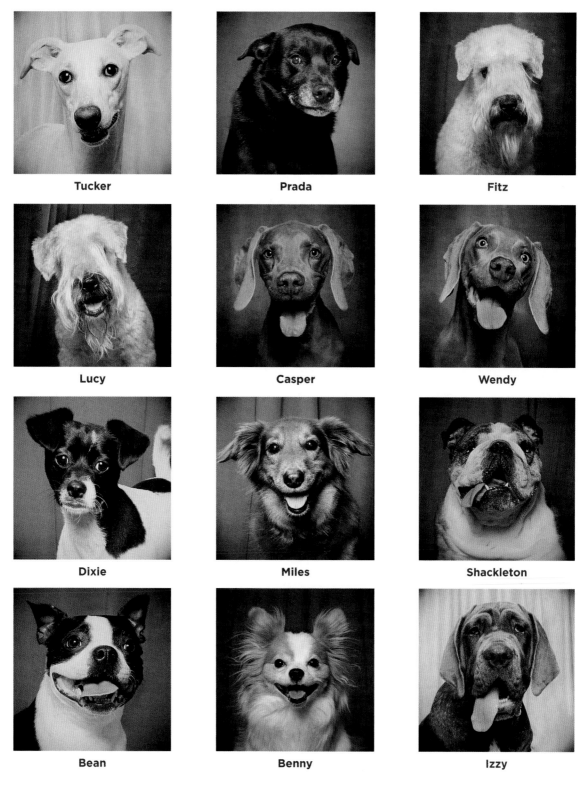

Tucker

Prada

Fitz

Lucy

Casper

Wendy

Dixie

Miles

Shackleton

Bean

Benny

Izzy

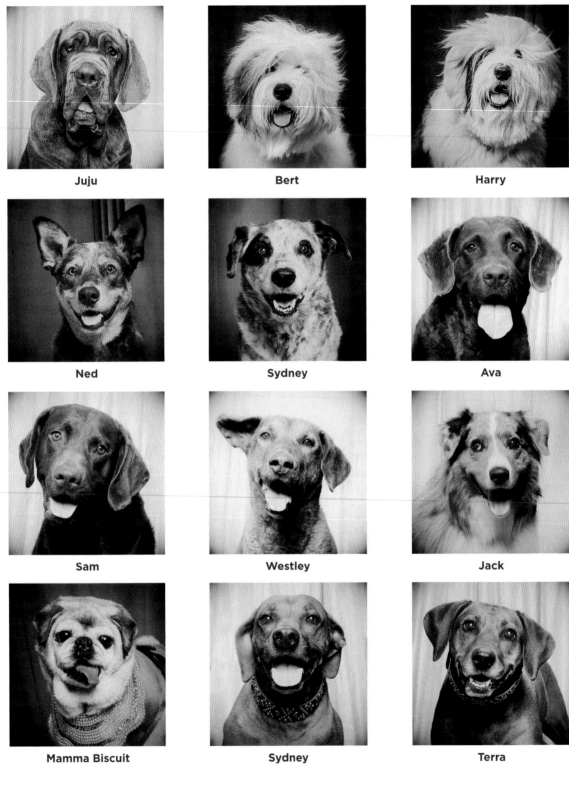

Juju

Bert

Harry

Ned

Sydney

Ava

Sam

Westley

Jack

Mamma Biscuit

Sydney

Terra

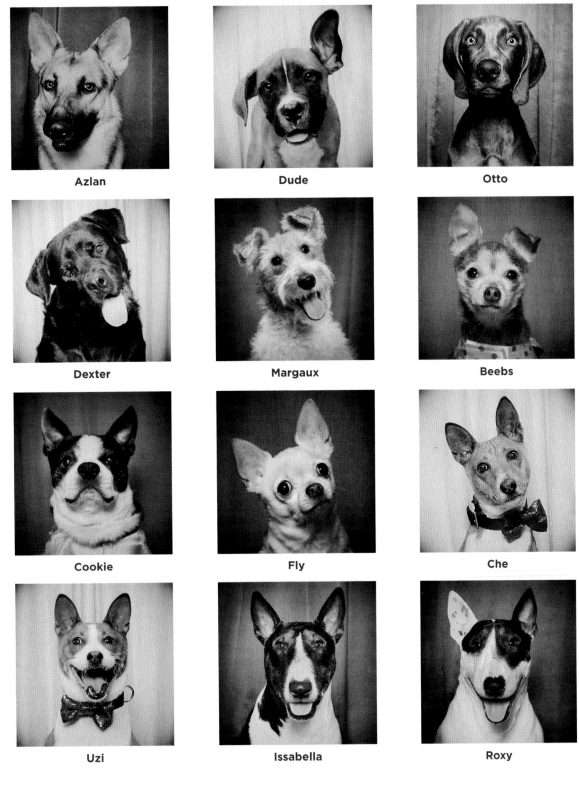

Azlan

Dude

Otto

Dexter

Margaux

Beebs

Cookie

Fly

Che

Uzi

Issabella

Roxy

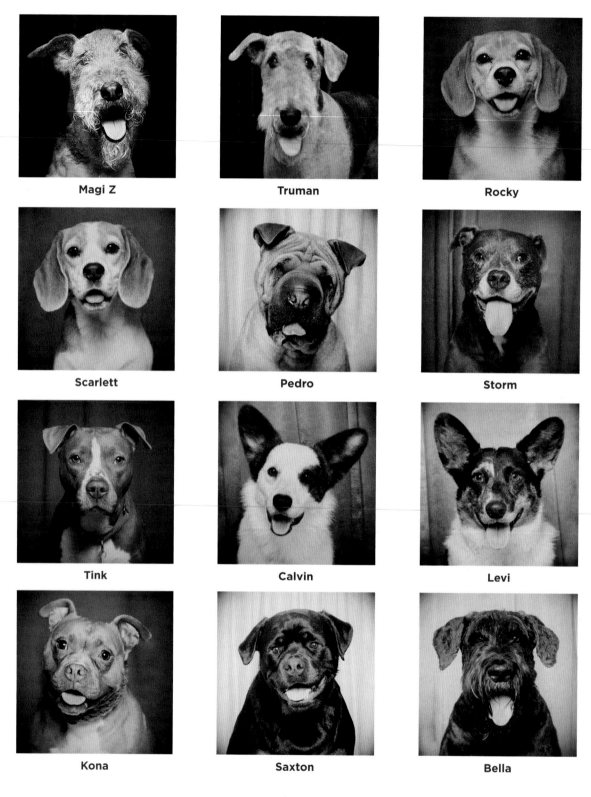

Magi Z

Truman

Rocky

Scarlett

Pedro

Storm

Tink

Calvin

Levi

Kona

Saxton

Bella

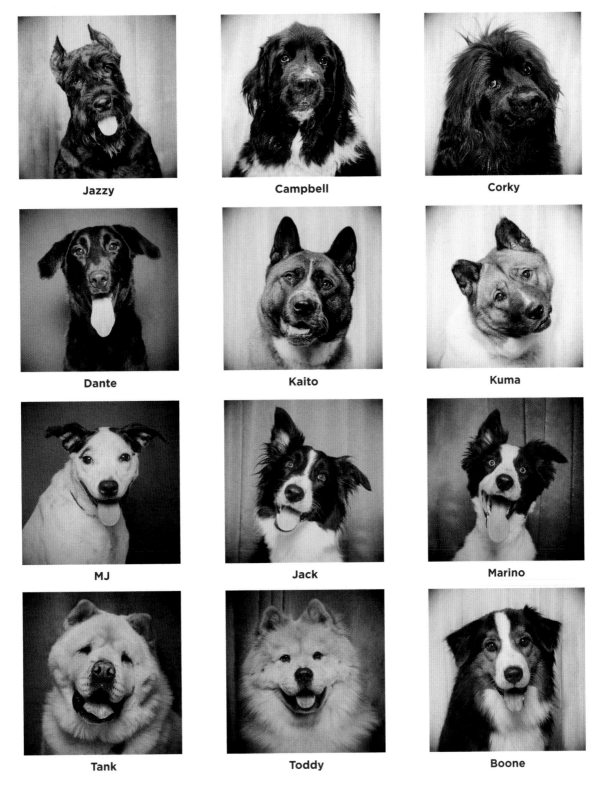

Jazzy

Campbell

Corky

Dante

Kaito

Kuma

MJ

Jack

Marino

Tank

Toddy

Boone

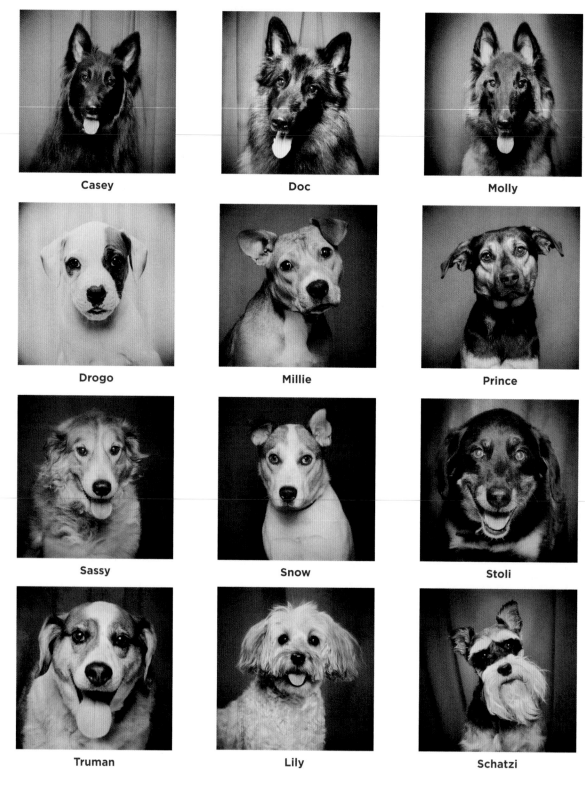

Casey

Doc

Molly

Drogo

Millie

Prince

Sassy

Snow

Stoli

Truman

Lily

Schatzi

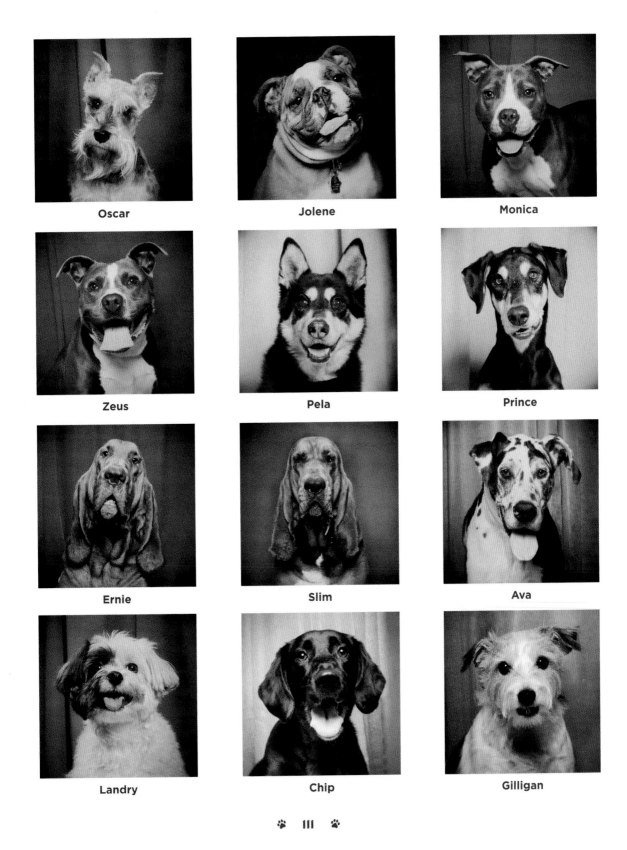

Oscar

Jolene

Monica

Zeus

Pela

Prince

Ernie

Slim

Ava

Landry

Chip

Gilligan

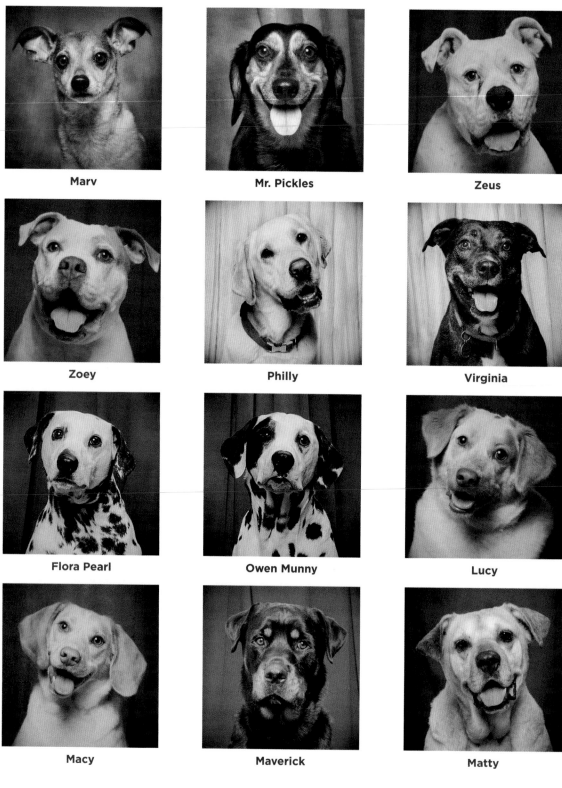

Marv

Mr. Pickles

Zeus

Zoey

Philly

Virginia

Flora Pearl

Owen Munny

Lucy

Macy

Maverick

Matty

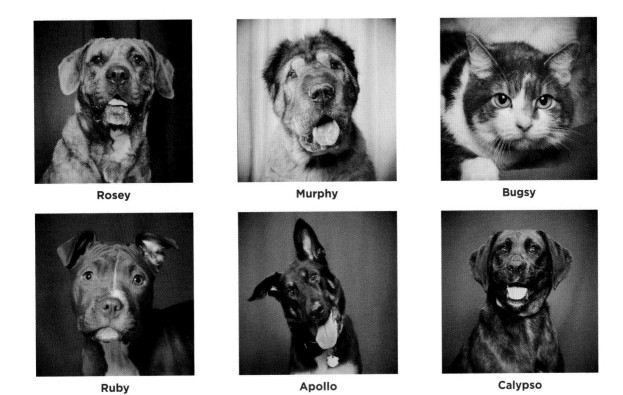

Rosey

Murphy

Bugsy

Ruby

Apollo

Calypso

ANIMAL WELFARE ORGANIZATIONS

APA (ANIMAL PROTECTIVE ASSOCIATION OF MISSOURI)
http://www.apamo.org/
CALL: (314) 645-4610
WRITE: 1705 South Hanley Road
St. Louis, MO 63144

ASPCA (AMERICAN SOCIETY FOR THE PREVENTION OF CRUELTY TO ANIMALS)
https://www.aspca.org/
CALL: (212) 876-7700
E-MAIL: through website
WRITE: American Society for the Prevention of Cruelty to Animals (ASPCA)
424 E. 92nd St
New York, NY 10128-6804

ATHLETES FOR ANIMALS
http://athletesforanimals.org/athletes/

GATEWAY PET GUARDIANS
http://www.gatewaypets.com/
CALL: (314) 664-7398
E-MAIL: info@gatewaypets.com
WRITE: P.O. Box 13243
St. Louis, MO 63157

BEST FRIENDS ANIMAL SOCIETY
http://www.bestfriends.org
CALL: (435) 644-2001
E-MAIL: info@bestfriends.org
WRITE: 5001 Angel Canyon Road
Kanab, UT 84741-5000

MUTTS-N-STUFF
http://www.muttsnstuff.com/
CALL: (314) 306-MUTT
E-MAIL: muttsnstuff@yahoo.com
WRITE: P.O. BOX 187
Foristell, MO 63348

NEADS (NATIONAL EDUCATION FOR ASSISTANCE DOG SERVICES)
http://www.neads.org/
CALL: (978) 422-9064
E-MAIL: info@neads.org
WRITE: 305 Redemption Rock Trail South
Princeton, MA 01541

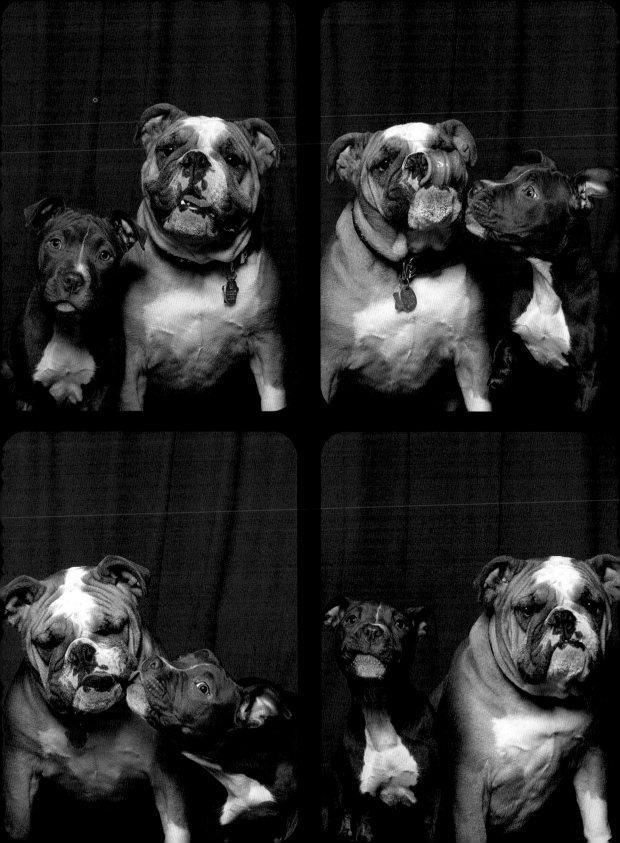

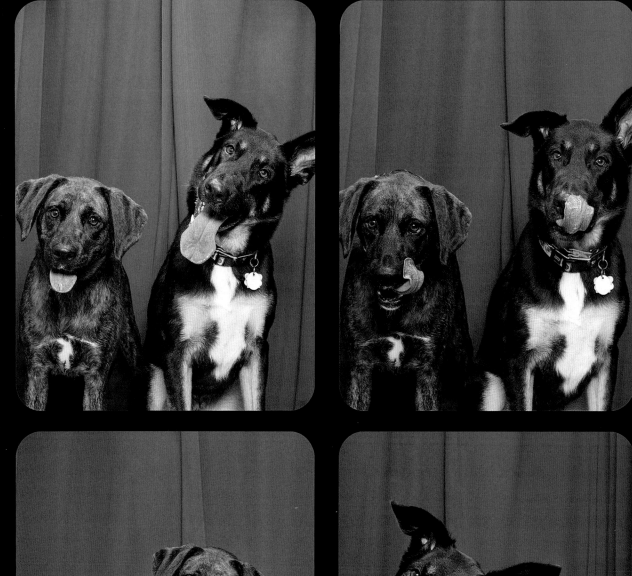

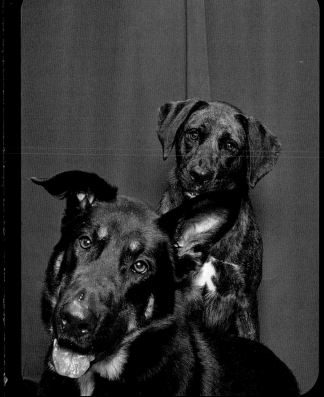
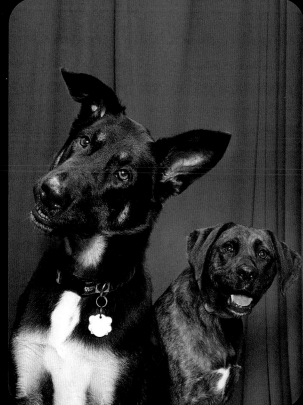

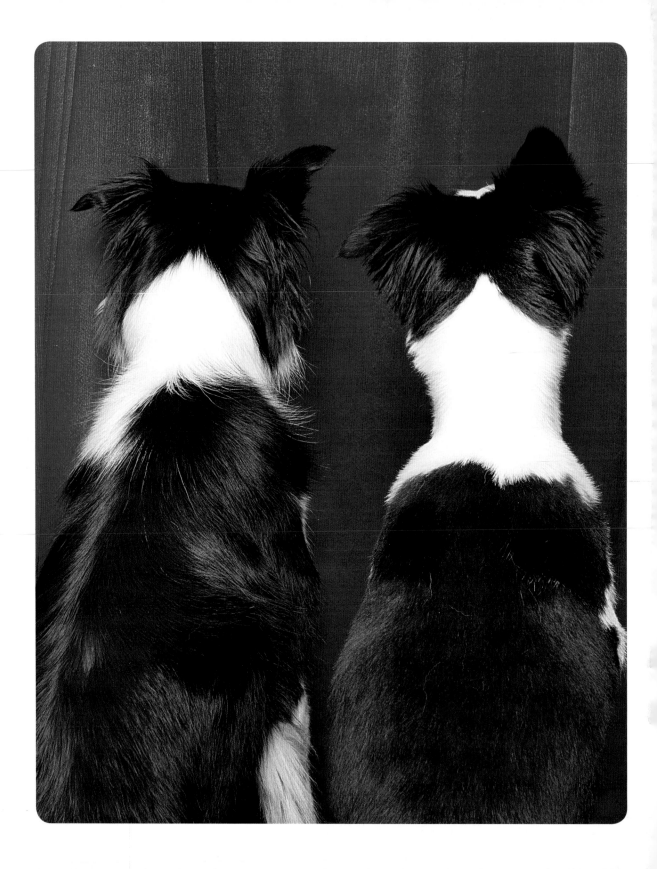